EVERY BUSH AFIRE

PRAISE FOR EVERY BUSH AFIRE

"Believing in God is one thing. Hearing from Him, quite another. But to entertain the baffling reality of His nearness—our oneness with God, in Christ, by the power of the Holy Spirit? That's the invitation waiting for you in this powerful book."

Brit Eaton
Author of *The Uncovery*

"Kyle Peters makes one truth crystal clear. God is on the move! Integrating stirring personal narrative with keen biblical insight, *Every Bush Afire* will awaken the reader to the manifest Presence of the Lord and open closed eyes to the movement of God's Kingdom in daily life."

Terry Wardle
Author of *Some Kind of Crazy*

"You will be stirred and inspired by Kyle's potent personal stories and real life testimonies of cultivating and walking in friendship with Jesus. I was struck by his ability to take the mystical and make it relatable. You'll be blessed by this message, ignited, and set aflame!"

Micah Level
Bestselling author of *Set Apart For Him*

EVERY BUSH AFIRE

Kyle Peters

Foreword by
Putty Putman

The Pearl
PEARLBOOKS.CO

Developmental Editor
BRAD PAUQUETTE

Copy Editor
THIRZAH GRIFFIOEN

Cover Designer
JESSICA OSTRANDER

Print ISBN: 978-1-960230-00-3
E-book ISBN: 978-1-960230-01-0

CONTENTS

To Melissa

You found the Treasure in the field, and you went after it without compromise. Your pursuit of the Presence and for deep healing was uncomfortable and offensive until it became catalytic. The way you relate to Jesus inspires me to go after more than I've known was available. Let's never stop breaking our boxes.

FOREWORD

EVERY ONE OF US LIVES a one-of-a-kind story; our unique history, passions, experiences, relationships, and dreams are ours alone. Our walk with God tells a narrative that unveils who God is in a way that no one else's life can reveal.

As we sojourn with the Lord, it is invaluable to be able to see the roads other believers have walked. Though our journey is our own, we walk with the same God. His love, encouragement, challenge, and guidance in each of our stories bear many of the same hallmarks. We each walk a different road, but in another respect we all walk the same way.

For this reason, an inside glimpse into someone else's journey can be an incredible asset to our own adventure. There are many examples of "highlights reels"—stories that focus on the mountain peaks of the journey, with decades summarized in a few chapters. These stories can portray the journey with a misleading texture: it seems like it's about fifteen minutes between each profound and life-changing experience.

Perhaps that is the journey for some, but my road hasn't worked that way. Yes, there are profound and powerful moments with God, but there are also long stretches of the road that have been challenging and painful. Walking with God hasn't erased confusion—rather it has often relocated it. I used to be confused about how the world works, now I am often confused about what God is up to and why! Pain has not left my life either, nor has loss or grief. Some days are mountain peaks, some days valleys, and many days I mostly just feel "normal"—filled with God, but empty of ecstatic experiences.

This has been the shape of my journey and I suspect it is the road we all travel. Learning to journey with God is a large part of the art of the adventure. Our God is the Lord of the mountain tops, the Victor of the valleys, and the ultimate Companion in utter normalcy. He loves it all and excels in every part.

Every Bush Afire is a beautiful and powerful book. It is an authentic and unblemished record of the full story of the adventure with God. Kyle takes us to the highest mountain peaks, sharing with us stories that will bring tears to your eyes as we see the heart of God made concrete in his beautiful works. With just as much clarity, Kyle marches us into the valleys—moments of intense grief, pain, or loss, in which God proves that He is the one who sticks closer than a brother. In these valley moments where the brokenness of life has left its fingerprints on our story, God shows us that He is the source of our wholeness.

Not content to leave it there, Kyle urges us forward, taking us along as he navigates the circumstances of life. Like yours, Kyle's life has been lived with the tensions and highlights of treasured relationships, job frustrations, and an uncertain future—through it all Kyle has walked with the Spirit of God as a constant companion.

What does a life lived with God look like? These pages carry a picture of the real thing. This is the texture you can expect. The details will be different in your adventure: the circumstances unique to you, but the essence of it—what it feels like to take that adventure—is captured beautifully here.

May this book inspire you to press forward into your own God-led adventure, may it authenticate the road the Lord has you on. May you, like Kyle, discover that with our God, every bush is afire with His glorious presence.

Putty Putman
Pastor, Author, Kingdom Pioneer

PROLOGUE

"Earth's crammed with heaven,
And every common bush afire with God,
But only he who sees takes off his shoes;
The rest sit round and pluck blackberries."
ELIZABETH BARRETT BROWNING

IN ONE SEASON OF HISTORY, the presence of God was limited to particular places, people, and times. Two craftsmen were filled with God's Spirit (Exodus 31:1-6), God chose to live in the tabernacle and the temple, and an occasional bush would catch fire (Exodus 3). But in this day and age, the Spirit has been poured out on all flesh (Acts 2), the veil between heaven and earth has been torn[1], and every bush is afire with God's presence.

---

1 This might sound dramatic, but it wasn't too dramatic for Mark. In his rendition of the Gospel, the word "torn" shows up in two significant moments. Like the other Gospel writers, Mark describes the curtain as being "torn from top to bottom" at the death of Jesus (15:38). He uses the same Greek work, *schizo*, at the baptism of Jesus. When the Spirit descended on Him, the heavens were torn open. This is a clear picture of a dramatic shift in recognition of Jesus: the space where God dwells is no longer distinct from where we live.

The Lord once spoke to me about the value of my experiences with Him. I stepped out of a wooded hillside into an open field. I walked through the field, looking down, taking note of the fleeting snow, exposing trampled grass. I happened to look down at the right time and noticed a shell. It caught my attention because it was so out of place. I picked it up, wondering out loud, "How in the world did this get here?" Without missing a beat, I heard the Lord respond, "The best things you have to give to others all come from your time with Me."

I laugh at the non-sequential nature of this experience as I think about it, but what He said became cemented in my mind. Not long after, I came across a verse that I had never noticed before. After telling several parables, Jesus said, "Therefore every scribe who has been trained for the kingdom of heaven is like a master of a house, who brings out of his treasure what is new and what is old." (Matthew 13:52) To be "trained in the kingdom" is to have a house full of treasure that can be brought out and shared with others. For me, there is no greater treasure than our history with God.

I want to share my treasure with you, and I want to position you to discover your own. You have your own stories.

You're on a journey, and its trajectory has a much more significant impact on the world around you than you're aware. The more fully you can step into an awareness of God's presence with you, the more equipped you are for your journey. I am convinced that your ability to navigate your destiny is directly correlated to your communion with the presence of God. You can learn to cultivate an intimate connection with Him, and to navigate daily challenges and decisions with Him in a way that immerses your world in His goodness.

I'm honored to walk with you.

This book is not the whole of my story, it's a snapshot. It takes place over a twelve-year period (so...maybe it's a panoramic snapshot). It begins with a miracle that initiates an unraveling. When faced with the reality of the nearness of God, my understanding of Him shifted. What I discovered is that when our understanding of God shifts, every other category of our lives is at risk of a massive upheaval.

These stories are my testimony to a God who walks with us. He calls us His beloved. He delights in us, He embraces us. He talks to us.

God speaks to us through as many avenues as we can imagine. Through scripture, through those around us, through dreams and visions. Sometimes He uses words, sometimes pictures or music, often when He speaks it feels like our thoughts. Sometimes His voice is big and loud, but more often it's subtle and easily overlooked.

Hearing His voice is something to be learned; our ability to hear His voice can grow with practice. This book is my personal invitation to you to walk with God as a way of life.

> You will make known to me the path of life;
> In your presence there is fullness of joy.
> PSALM 16:11

My hope is that as you read these stories, you'll discover a world saturated with the presence of God and you'll walk away with an increased capacity to discern His movements.

CHAPTER 1
NEARER THAN I KNEW

"*¿CÓMO SE DICE…*" I mimed taking a drink. I sat there, on stone bleachers in a Guatemalan village, waiting for the answer from local ten-year-olds. They looked at each other and laughed, much like the way they laughed as they watched me play *fútbol*. Running around a field with a bunch of small people is a different experience when you're this close to the equator, and I was thirsty. As a young youth pastor, I felt like I was a bit over my head leading our group on an international mission trip.

Our language training for this trip consisted of learning the most important words, such as "*¿dónde está el baño*?" We were also taught a strategy, which I deployed often, to say the phrase *"cómo se dice"* ("how do you say…") and then to mime what you are trying to say. It's quite entertaining…for the locals.

"*Cerveza*!" answered one of the ornerier looking boys. The others were wide-mouthed and laughing, a younger girl smacked her cheeks and squealed. I had no idea what was so funny. I proudly declared, "*Mi ami cerveza*."

The kids burst out laughing as they ran their separate ways. I was certain I had clearly communicated my request. It wasn't until later that evening that I was able to ask the translator about it. Apparently, I had made more than one mistake. The most apparent being that I identified myself as "beer" to a group of children.

That week we were privileged to stay right next to Lake Atitlán, with its crystal clear water, surrounded by several villages settled in the midst of the mountains. The little streets were littered with vendors and bike-taxis, many of which were decorated with murals of the late Michael Jackson—who had died less than a month before we arrived. When our bus first pulled into town, the kids at the front ran for the nearest vendor, eager to treat themselves to local food.

They were also the first of the group to familiarize themselves with *el baños*, but eventually the diarrhea plague hit almost all of us. Only two of us remained unscathed by the sickness that seemed to be targeting the foreigners. On day four, as a few of the leaders began to get sick, Chuck came to my room. One of our volunteer leaders, he stood in the doorway in shorts and a polo, leaning on his cane. With a stern voice he said, "Come with me."

As a young leader in this crew, I was sure I was in trouble. Chuck was one of those guys with big hands and a crushing handshake. He was going to give me a piece of his mind.

I followed him off the property, into the village night. The cool air of the night was a relief after hot, humid days. Patiently, I watched as he limped the steady incline to a nearby 7-Eleven. I followed him into the store, and watched as he grabbed two cans of *cerveza* and took them to the register. Without saying a word, he handed one to me and led me out to a bench overlooking the scene beyond.

The narrow stone streets of the village curved into mayhem, with small storefronts packed tight along the lane that snaked up the steep incline at the base of a mountain. Below us, just a few hundred yards away, the mountain met the lake, with mountains on every side. The lake was such an odd contrast to the mountains. It was so still and silent. A picture of peace in the midst of wild, jagged peaks.

Chuck took a seat on the bench and waited for me to join him. He opened his can and gestured for me to follow suit.

He took a sip; I took a sip.

"I'm one of the only ones left who hasn't gotten sick yet. Do you know why?" He pointed his finger at the beer in my hand. "Every night so far, I've walked to that 7-Eleven and gotten one of these. I think it's helping my stomach."

I had no clue whether his theory could be accurate, but I liked it.

Up until recently, I didn't know you could drink alcohol and be a Christian. I am very thankful for my upbringing, but I was trained to believe that the Bible said, "Don't drink, don't smoke, don't chew, and don't go with girls who do."

My first beer was about a year ago, at 10 a.m. on a golf course with my boss/pastor. His love for Jesus was so real and evident that I eventually opened myself to the possibility that alcohol wasn't the evil I had been told it was. I had two beers and a braut that day. It was heavenly.

After that evening on the streetside bench, Chuck and I enjoyed a beer together after our nightly team meetings. We never made it to the beer on the final night. The crew met out on the porch to debrief from our final day. Pastor Antonio, the local hosting pastor, was at the center of discussion. Earlier in the day he told us stories that were...hard to believe.

He told a story about some vandals who had broken into the church and stolen some sound equipment. He had led the church in praying for the men for a few weeks. In a series of odd circumstances, he had the opportunity to help the men when they were in trouble and they gave their lives to Jesus. Then the stories grew stranger. He began to tell stories of people being healed on the spot and visible angels intervening in life-threatening situations.

In one story, a young mother from the village interrupted an evening service, sobbing at the doorway. Antonio handed the service to someone, then stepped out of their small concrete building along with an American missionary who was visiting. The young mother was holding her baby, whose skin had turned an unnatural color. The missionary happened to be a doctor, he checked the baby and pronounced it dead. Antonio began to pray boldly for the baby. For over thirty minutes the three of them stood outside of the church, calling for a miracle. Antonio felt prompted to bring the baby inside and have the whole church pray. Within moments of the church gathering around, the baby revived.

Under the stars our team huddled in a circle on the porch. It was clear that they were all shaken from the stories we had heard.

One of the younger students spoke up first.

"Does this kind of stuff *actually* happen?"

"Absolutely." I stroked my beard, hoping to appear intelligent. "Miracles happen all the time. We just don't hear about them as often, because they don't fit our Western–"

Suddenly, Chuck slammed his Bible on the ground in front of him. The group went silent. "For sixteen years I have had multiple sclerosis." Chuck looked around the circle, tears swelling. "Why hasn't God healed *me*!"

I knew it was good for Chuck to get out his grief, so I didn't want to answer too quickly. But in the silence I was formulating an answer. This wouldn't be a debate; we would minister comfort to Chuck. We would tell him it would be ok as we pat him on the back, then we would pray. I was already creating a prayer that Chuck would see his limp as a blessing, just like Jacob after he wrestled with God.

"I think we should pray for Chuck to be healed." Deb's voice cut through the silence. The group looked in her direction. Her daughter was barely old enough to join this trip, so Deb came along as a leader. She was sitting across the circle from me. She was leaning back, with her hands facing up, resting on her lap. She had short, dark hair and she was wearing a dress.

Deb never wore dresses. In fact, she had to buy some specifically for this trip. It was a requirement since people dress up for church in this culture. It was funny seeing her in a dress now, she was not the type. She was a wild card with a loud personality. I had heard stories of Deb swinging on vines and driving her minivan into wet cement. I had faithfully attended Tuesday night prayer group under her leadership. I admit, I was learning so much about prayer by simply being around her.

But now this?

She stayed calm, but raised her voice. "I'm serious. Chuck, I think God wants to heal you."

Chuck responded, "I'd like that."

Many of the teens began to lean forward, rubbing their hands together. I'd never seen a group of teens so excited for a prayer time. As the group began to pray, the energy on the porch rose. These Presbyterian teens began to pray bold prayers for God to heal. At first I was so concerned. The last thing I wanted was a bunch of disappointed kids, questioning their faith when nothing resulted from their prayers. But the momentum couldn't be stopped, and it was starting to have an effect on me as well.

We prayed for more than two hours. There was electricity in the atmosphere. I began to have a sense that this was more than our enthusiasm, I wondered if God was visiting our little gathering. Throughout the prayer time I noticed Deb would say something like, "I have a sense that we need to…" or "I think the Lord is saying…"

Each time she did, the anticipation rose higher. We had spontaneous worship more than once, and several kids expressed a renewed passion for Jesus. Around midnight it finally slowed and we dispersed to our rooms.

I walked into my room wide-eyed, replaying the last few hours in my mind. Then there was a knock on the door. I opened it to find Ramsey, one of the students, standing there, lighting a cigarette with shaking hands. Ramsey had always made it clear that he was not a believer, his mom made him come on the trip. As he put the cigarette to his mouth, I noticed his hand was shaking.

"What the hell was that, man?" he asked.

Smoking was clearly a breach in the agreement for attending the trip, but I didn't care at this point. I almost wanted to ask him if he had an extra. "I honestly don't know!" I paused, watching him as he turned toward the lake, puffing smoke toward the sky. "I mean, I think it was God."

"That was totally God right?" He looked down, his cigarette lit up as he inhaled again. He shook his head. "It can't be God."

"What do you mean? Why not?"

"Because, if there's a God, it means I'd be held accountable to him."

I was speechless.

Our experience demanded we reassess our understanding of God. What's funny is at this point, we had given little to no thought as to whether Chuck was healed. He still had a limp, so maybe we thought it was a wash? But we had just had a real encounter with supernatural power. God had shown up in a way that caused me to question the way I had understood him.

I wouldn't have said it, but up until that point, God had been a distant concept, not a present reality.

My mind was reeling on the flight home as the questions continued to bubble up.

"Kyle."

I turned my head, Chuck was a few rows behind me, across the aisle, waving me over. I walked over. Calmly, Chuck said, "I think I'm having a stroke."

"Huh?" I had no idea how to respond. His calm was disorienting. "How do you know?"

"My left side is numb."

"Okay." I followed suit and kept calm. Up the aisle was a stewardess. I approached her. "Excuse me, I think someone might be having a stroke."

She didn't share my calm. Immediately she yelled, "Is there a doctor on the plane?"

A hand raised toward the front of the plane. The man stood and walked back to the two of us. "What's the problem?"

I pointed at Chuck. "He said his left side is numb."

The doctor asked Chuck a few questions. "Well we can't know for sure, but it seems you're having a stroke. Take some aspirin and let's have an ambulance ready at the gate." The stewardess moved us to first class so we could get off the plane quickly in Atlanta.

For the remainder of the flight my head was a whirlwind. *That's the last time I'll pray for someone to be healed!* I was sure we had made the mistake of making demands of God. It seemed odd after our experience that this would be unrelated, but how? Would God really do this? I didn't believe Him to be a sadist.

Deb came and visited us. "How are you guys doing?"

Chuck responded, "I'm fine." His tone told us he wasn't fine. He didn't seem in pain, but it was clear he was embarrassed. He had made it clear during the trip that he didn't want to be a burden, and now here he was.

"Hey, I've always wanted to fly first class Chuck, you've made my dream come true."

He gave a forced laugh.

Deb started to head back, I jumped up to follow her. "Deb... isn't it odd that this happened the day after we had an intense prayer time for him?"

"I know. I've been wondering about that too. The Lord keeps reminding me of Isaiah 26:3. Read it when you get back to your seat, you need it right now."

I was eager to see what it was about. I returned to my seat and opened my Bible.

"You keep him in perfect peace
Whose mind is stayed on you,
Because he trusts in you."

Well it's not talking about me, I'm definitely not in perfect peace. Then the thought occurred to me, *this is an invitation. You can be at peace, even now.*

So I prayed, *Okay Lord. I trust you. I trust that you are here. You care for Chuck and you care for me. Show me what you're doing now.*

When the plane landed Chuck and I were escorted off the plane, into the ambulance, bypassing customs entirely. While the rest of our crew caught the connecting flight home, Chuck and I spent the next five days in a hospital in Atlanta. We bonded over food from vending machines, interrupted sleep, and cheesy jokes with the nurses. After long waits and multiple tests, the doctor gave a diagnosis.

"Well I have bad news and good news. The bad news, you did have a stroke, and we're going to have a treatment plan moving forward."

Chuck and I exchanged curious looks. Chuck asked, "And the good news?"

"The good news," The doctor's eyes widened as he looked back at his clipboard. "Is that I find no evidence of MS in your system. I recommend you schedule an appointment when you get home to verify this with your doctor."

Chuck and I exchanged looks of disbelief.

"Ha! Ha!" Chuck hollered. He pointed his fist toward me. I took the invitation and gave him a fist-bump, forgetting the IV between his knuckles.

"Ow!"

"Oh man I'm sorry!"

He looked at me, laughing. His face was bright with delight.

God had visited that porch in Guatemala, we had witnessed an impossibility.

Chuck's wife arrived not long after and relieved me of my duties. On the flight home I watched the clouds move swiftly by my window as I considered the implications for my own life. A few weeks later Chuck would tell us that he met with the original three doctors who had diagnosed him sixteen years before. They would change his diagnosis from MS to something that looked like MS, but without the ongoing effects. That was evidence enough for me.

FUNCTIONAL DEISM

This was the beginning of an unraveling for me. I would soon discover that I was drinking Kool-Aid under the brand of Christianity that tasted more like deism. I believed in a God that was far off. He had created the world, sure. But then He stepped back, watching from somewhere else as the gears and cogs moved about. He would not be involved in the workings of my life, He would watch with a scowl and notate all the wrong moves that He knew I'd make. If He's a father, I'm an orphan.

I was among the *very religious* men in Athens that Paul addressed. I was worshiping *an unknown god.* My experience in Guatemala was one among many experiences where I was discovering that God "is actually not far from each one of us." (Acts 17:27) Like most of the Western Church, I had learned to filter out the supernatural events of the Bible. Of course some couldn't be filtered—like the resurrection, but I could comfortably keep those things separated 2,000 years from my world.

Now a new world had been opened up to me. At its very core, it was a world in which God's presence could be experienced, His voice could be heard, His affection could be felt. Up to this point I would say that the goal of my life was to please God. That would no longer be the aim of my life. I longed to know Him, personally. I had been handed a new map with a new heading, in a land with which I was largely unfamiliar. It awaited my exploration.

CHAPTER 2
THIN PLACES

IN THIS EXPLORATION PROCESS, I have found one muscle to be profoundly significant: awareness.

If God is nearer than I know, then my goal is *not* to get Him to come nearer, it's to *recognize* His nearness. So then the question becomes, "What are the activities and spaces which increase my awareness of God's presence?"

The air was much cooler at the top of the mountain. The last half mile of trail was nearly straight upwards over rocky terrain with several switchbacks. The others were still climbing. My anticipation had driven me to nearly run up the incline. At the top, I could see the trail opened up about a hundred yards ahead. The thick of the wood ended abruptly, met by a level field covered in blueberry bushes. To my right, a young bear was surprised to see me emerge. He took off in the other direction.

I took off my pack and surveyed the scene. *Breathed Mountain.* I could see how it earned its name. The wild wind of the higher elevation was tamed by the pines that surrounded the meadow. The air was crisp. I could almost feel the purity of the atmosphere, coursing through my body, offering healing to my soul, which was weary from the chaos of civilization.

Years ago, Deb had given me profound advice. I was burnt out. She passed me in the hallway of the church, the fatigue evident on my face. At the time I was a full-time student with a full-time job on third shift, two small kids at home, and volunteering as a youth pastor. I was burnt toast.

"You okay?" she asked.

I gritted my teeth. "I don't know how much longer I can keep this up." I admitted that I hated leading the teens, I felt like such a hypocrite. I wasn't experiencing connection with God, "Who am I to encourage others to do it?"

"You know what you need?"

I rolled my eyes, ready for the spiritual reprimand. "To read my Bible? To pray?"

"No. You need to go backpacking."

My eyes went wide. "Huh?"

"Spiritual practices are about positioning us to encounter God, right? Prayer and scripture have their place, for sure. But, Kyle, you come alive when you're hiking. The Lord loves that about you, and He loves to meet you in the wilderness. You need to plan a trip soon."

It had not been at all what I expected. But I didn't think it would fly with my wife.

Melissa and I had been married for about seven years, with two small children now in the picture. Since we started having kids our relationship had struggled. It wasn't the strain of caring for kids that caused the problems, although we certainly felt ill-equipped for their demands. There's something about having kids that brings to the surface all your unprocessed trauma.

When I told Melissa, her response was just as shocking. I expected her to be repulsed at the idea of me leaving for a few days. I wasn't home enough as it was. We sat on the edge of the hill behind our house, watching the kids as they ran in circles in the backyard.

"You should do it! You do need it."

"Are you serious?"

"Yeah." She was looking down, digging in the dirt with her finger. "I mean, I need you home more, but you're not really here when you are here. It's like your soul is disconnected from your body."

My face reddened.

Her eyes softened as she studied me for a moment. "Backpacking is your zipper," she exclaimed playfully.

I looked at her sideways, unable to hide the smile beginning to form. "What d'you mean?"

"You're becoming a little unzipped—your soul and your body, that is. You need to go backpacking to get zipped back up." She poked my belly button and pressed a line up to my chest, "Zzzzzzip!"

It didn't take long to get a hike on the books. There's a handful of guys who have ventured out into the wilderness with me over the years. Despite our many mishaps and missed turns they have continued to come along. We set our course and hit the road.

My heart was filled with gratitude as we explored the broad mountaintop over the next five miles. I may not have been hearing God speak to me, but I had such a heightened awareness of His presence on Breathed Mountain.

Somehow on the trail I become so much nearer to His heart. His joy radiates over me. His beauty envelopes me.

As we passed from open meadow to a pine sanctuary, to rocky outcropping, I was aware of not only His majesty, but just how near

He really was. *This is a thin place for me.*

THIN PLACES

Thanks to Saint Patrick and the missionaries that followed, Ireland is known for its holy sites. The people of Ireland coined the term "thin places," where heaven and earth seem to intersect. For Ireland, most of her thin places are not in centuries old cathedrals. They are in the hills and on the cliffs, beside lakes and along the shoreline. The veil between two worlds is at its thinnest in these places. It's common that the places that earn this title carry the rich history of those who have gone before us, who have told of their encounters with God there.

Bethel was such a place for Jacob and his family. Laying his head on a rock, he dreamed of angels ascending and descending between heaven and earth, and he received a promise from God himself. When he awoke, he said, "How awesome is this place! This is none other than the house of God, the gate of heaven." (Genesis 28:17) Several times for Jacob and his descendants, Bethel was a place to encounter God.

Thin places can be anywhere. They could be on a mountain or in the grocery store, on a drive through the country or in your family room. When we have an experience where we become aware of God's presence, our history becomes a testimony. Whenever we step into those places of past encounters, our memory sparks the same awareness and positions us for new encounters.

THE ORIGINAL THIN PLACE

The Garden in Genesis 2 is the original thin place. More than farmland to be cultivated, the Garden was a resting place for God to visit the earth. He would visit Adam and Eve in the Garden, and walk with them in the cool of the day. God set humanity in the Garden because He intended to have intimate fellowship with them. In fact, it's this place of intimacy with God that Adam and Eve were told to cultivate and grow.

The whole earth was meant to be a thin place, and the Garden was the starting point. Paul told us that Jesus is going to unite all things in heaven and earth (Ephesians 1:10). In Colossians 1:20 he used the word *reconcile* to describe this, which tells us that heaven and earth were once united. The Garden was that union between heaven and earth. Humanity's job was to cultivate that union; to value it and to grow it.

I like to imagine that the wilderness is my garden. It's so easy to connect with God on the trail. I go for a few days, soaking in His presence, and I come home with handfuls of rich nutrients, seeking to plant the awareness of His presence in my living room, in the coffee shop, and in the church. I have a heightened sense of Him that infects my world with the reality of His goodness. I've discovered that the best thing I have to give to others comes from the intimacy I've cultivated with Him. While I can't imagine a better meeting place with God than the wilderness, others encounter God much closer to home.

Melissa has developed thin places all over our house. When I worked third shift, she would get giddy as I left for work. She would get the babies to bed, do some quick cleaning, then spend time in worship in the living room. She regularly told me stories of encounters with God on the floor. She would see angels in the room, hear God speaking to her heart, and sometimes have out-of-body experiences in the spirit. I would be lying if I said I was never weirded out when she would tell me about her experiences.

She admits it wasn't that way at first. For the first few months she would binge-watch her favorite shows, go to bed late into the night, then wake up the next morning exhausted and depressed. One day she decided that it wasn't working. Out of desperation for something to change, she made a different decision and started spending time in worship. A deep hunger for intimacy with God began to stir in her.

A NEW THIN PLACE

Nathaniel had a thin place experience in John 1. When Phillip came to tell him about Jesus, he responded with skepticism. "Can anything good come out of Nazareth?"

To his surprise, Jesus greeted him with personal knowledge about him. With his jaw dropped, Nathaniel responded, "How do you know me?" Jesus's intimate knowledge was enough to convince Nathaniel that Jesus is no ordinary man.

You can almost hear Jesus laughing as he responded, "You will see heaven opened, and the angels of God ascending and descending on the Son of Man." (John 1:43-51)

Interesting choice of words Jesus used. Jesus is reminding us of the story of Jacob's encounter at Bethel. What had been a location previously, Jesus applied to himself. **The very person of Jesus is a thin place.** He is now the meeting place between heaven and earth. Everyone he encounters is given an opportunity for an encounter with God. Everywhere he steps becomes a thin place.

This changes the nature of thin places for the believer. Thin places are not limited to geographical spaces. In John 17, Jesus prayed a prayer that again initiated the assignment of the Garden for humanity.

I do not ask for these only,
but also for those who will believe in me through their word,
that they may all be one, just as you, Father, are in me, and I in you,
That they also may be in us
So that the world may believe that you have sent me.

And just like that, we were plopped back into the place we belong, the place of intimate fellowship with God. Except this time, it's not a location, it's a person. Jesus has become our home address; he's the place where we live. You are fully at rest in Him right now. Now, we don't look for thin places, we cultivate the Garden within us. Our awareness and connection with God's presence within us enables us to cultivate thin places everywhere we go.

My prayer for you, as you read these stories, is that your world would be infused with thin places. I want to give you some of my stories as an appetizer. I hope that as you read them, your heart is stirred with hunger for more of the Lord. As Peter found out in the house of Cornelius, God does not show favoritism (Acts 10:34). When you hear stories of God moving in someone else's life, the same is available for you. If you're feeling dangerous, take a breath and pray the following prayer…

God, give me thin places!
I want to experience your nearness and encounter your realness.
I am not satisfied with knowing about you. I want to know you more personally.
Lead me to places, people, and circumstances that will position me to see heaven intersect with earth.

CHAPTER 3

THINNER SPACES

I CLIMBED THE SIX-FOOT LADDER to the top of the narrow closet. I took a breath and squeezed through the attic entrance. The rafters were barely wide enough, with the angled roof nine inches above the rafters. It was a miracle I made it through, dragging the six-inch-wide hose behind me. My father-in-law is a handyman. Somehow he managed to sweet-talk me into being his attic monkey, squeezing into dark, dusty attics and filling them with insulation.

Most of the jobs were with fiberglass—a fluffy, pink material that falls like a gentle snow. Sometimes however, we used cellulose—a recycled material ground up into piles of dust. Coming full speed out of the tube, it's less like a gentle snow and more like a violent sandstorm. Unfortunately, this attic was going to be cellulose. I barely had room to move without jamming my head into a nail piercing down through the roof or falling through the ceiling between rafters.

I became more and more terrified as I set up to blow. I squeezed as far as I could down a narrow section of the attic, crawling over and under duct work.

How am I going to get out? Once I start blowing, I'll be blind.

My breathing shallowed. *I don't think I'm getting out. This is where I die.* I could feel the space closing in on me. *They're going to find my body years from now! There's not enough air up here.*

At this last thought, a gust of wind shot up through the access panel, hitting me in the back of the head. I gave a nervous laugh. I could sense the Lord's response to my panic.

Kyle, there's more than enough of what you need, even here.

"Are you sure, Lord?"

I promise.

Courage filled me. I became more aware of the space around me than the enclosures, the attic seemed to expand before me. I reached for the remote, pushing the button to send the material. As the sandstorm began to brew I gave a maniacal laugh for no one in particular. In my best pirate voice, I announced to the attic, "Aye, we have all the space we need lads!"

If thin places are certain sites with a rich history of encounter, "thinner spaces" are the places of pressure, where I have the privilege of releasing the presence of God that I carry. Thinner spaces are the spaces in our lives where pressure and panic threaten to crush us, but we learn to push back with the conscious reality of Christ in us. Thinner spaces are the crises that threaten to overcome us, but instead of giving into fear, we choose to engage with God's presence in such a way that alters the crisis.

"Do you replace water heaters?" a friend of mine asked.

"Sure!"

The truth was, I'd never done anything with water heaters, besides relighting a pilot light. But I had decided that I was willing to take some risks, and step into things I've never tried before. YouTube would be all the training I needed.

Wes came with me to purchase the new water heater. I had first met Wes when he was in prison. He had left a significant impression on me in his blue jumpsuit and genuine smile. He opened up about the shame he was working through, and his deepening awareness of God's love. He was learning to be fully real and unreserved before God. As I listened to him, watching the prison yard through the window behind him, I saw a level of freedom and security that I longed for. By the time he got out a year later, I had visited him several times, for my own benefit.

The two of us carried the water heater down the steep staircase and set it next to the old one.

Wes asked, "Do you need anything else before I go?"

"No, man, I've got it from here!"

He left in a hurry, he had a busy day ahead of him. As I turned to the task at hand, I realized my mistake. The water heater that I bought was electric, and what I was replacing was gas. I hung my head. My internal temperature rose ten degrees as I considered the cost of my mistake. I kicked myself thinking about how my family's finances were too tight for such a costly mistake.

I started to ask, "Will I even make any money on this job when all is said and done?"

As if in direct response to my question, the Lord spoke to my heart. I could sense His laughter as He said, "You're not doing this to provide, that's my job. You're doing this because I made you like me, your work is an expression of who you are."

In a moment it was like the weight of a heavy water heater was lifted off of my chest. Provision was not dependent upon my ability to succeed; my Dad would take care of me. So I was freed up to solve the problem and finish the job not out of fear, but out of a heart and a mind like my Dad. If He believed in me, then I'd conquer this problem, and I wouldn't have to do it alone.

"Okay Dad, how are we going to solve this one?" I asked, as I climbed the basement steps for fresh air.

Suddenly I heard '90s rock in the distance, and I pictured a young muscular guy available to give me a hand. I walked down the alley, and sure enough, all tatted up with his shirt off, a young buck was detailing a truck. He helped me lift the water heater out of the basement with his pinky, and I was off for the right water heater. When I returned, he helped me carry it down, and we had a great conversation about recovery and some wicked good prayer time.

Did you know that in the story of the Creation, work came *before* the Fall? Work is not a curse, it's a gift. Work is only a curse when we fall for the lie that we are abandoned and alone. Work is a thinner space, where we impact the world as we learn to co-create with Him. The Garden was Adam and Eve's workplace. It was the canvas for God and humanity to create together.

Work is not a curse, work is glory. Like the Garden, our work is a space where we can rely on Him, asking for solutions to problems. Work is a space where we can lean into heavenly wisdom, bringing heaven more fully to earth. Your work is a place where you can learn to join God in His creative self-expression.

God himself enjoys work, it's how He expresses Himself. He shows off His creativity, His genius, His beauty, His generosity, His power. Take note of anyone you see working today. They are showing you something of the nature of God. They were given that capacity, and we wouldn't see it if not for work.

Work is not the only thinner space we experience. Think of the challenging circumstances of your own story. Ever find yourself in the midst of chaos, where things are out of your control? How about those moments of disappointment or utter failure? Because of God's ridiculous capacity for redemption, these moments can become thinner places, where pressure is faced with Presence.

I had met Mitch nearly a year before, when he began attending our School of Kingdom Ministry class. SoKM was a class held once a week, equipping people for a *naturally supernatural lifestyle.*

Mitch came in wearing his Green Bay Packers jersey and jeans. He had a soft smile, and he towered over us at six foot two. Mitch and I quickly became fast friends, sharing cheesy humor and obnoxious pranks. His gentle spirit combined with his deep voice caused his laughter to radiate through you when he brought you in for a hug.

When SoKM ended that May, he asked to meet me for coffee. I walked into the Meeting Grounds to discover Mitch managing the coffee shop. As I approached, Mitch smiled at me from behind the counter. "Let me make you my favorite drink!"

I sat and watched. Mitch was clearly loved by the staff around him. The crew exchanged playful banter between those up front and those in the back. Mitch moved with grace among them, connecting and affirming as he gave direction. He seemed in his element. He finished my drink and joined me at the table.

As he sat, he handed me my drink. "I've got one question for you."

"Let's hear it."

"Are you doing SoKM again this Fall?"

"I'm not sure. Probably."

He narrowed his eyes, "Kyle. You have to do it again. People need to experience this." He shook his head as he looked down at his drink, then back up again. "The teaching on identity, alone, was exactly what I needed at exactly the right time. If you're not going to do it, then tell me how I can do it. I don't care to lead it, I just need to go through it again."

The class had revolutionized the way he viewed himself, and it was causing a radical shift in his relationship with the Lord. Mitch was all the evidence I needed to continue with SoKM. In fact, during that conversation I invited him to join the leadership team. He became our promoter. I wonder how many people came through SoKM over the years because of his testimony.

Just a few months later, Mitch walked into our church building with his head down. He surveyed the space, "Is there anywhere private we could talk?"

I led him to the nursery. Without saying a word, he grabbed a small pillow from the crib. He went to the floor, curled into a ball, and sobbed into the pillow. I wanted to ask him what was wrong, I wanted to alleviate whatever this was. It was uncomfortable. And yet, there was something holy taking place. I found some soft instrumental music on my phone, then leaned back into the rocking chair and prayed silent prayers.

This went on for at least thirty minutes. At first I felt so helpless. *What is someone supposed to do here?* But I began to realize, he simply needed someone to witness his grief. What a sacred privilege. I imagine that if, out of my discomfort, I would have made him interact with me, this necessary process would have been stopped short. I believe that my mere presence in the room was representative of God's nearness. God was seeing his pain, and I was a signpost to that reality. I hadn't a clue what the loss was, and I didn't need to know.

The sobs shifted from constant to spurts. Then his breathing began to slow. He was quiet. After a few minutes of silence, I asked, "Are you able to tell me what's going on?"

He studied me with red, swollen eyes. "She left me. She's gone, for good." The sobs returned for a moment.

All I wanted to do was reassure him. *I'm sure she'll be back. This will get worked out, your marriage will be fine!* But I hadn't a clue. I waited in silence, hoping for more information.

He looked up at me again, studying my face. "There's a lot you don't know about me, Kyle."

"Like what?"

"Well, did you know I was incarcerated for nine years?"

My eyes widened. "I had no idea."

"I've struggled with some sick stuff." He closed his eyes and shook his head towards the carpet. He continued, "Well a few months ago I relapsed. I didn't tell Jess, and she found out. Now she's done."

My heart sank. As shameful as it was, I'm no stranger to brokenness. In fact, I don't know anyone who is. Here Mitch was, so bound up in it that he was experiencing new levels of drastic consequences.

Our conversation went in spurts, with sobs in between, the music always in the background. There would be a long and painful process ahead of him, but Mitch experienced the Father's heart in that nursery. He was accepted and dearly loved.

Over the weeks, months and years that followed, I was among the few who were privileged to walk with him in his journey. That dark day propelled Mitch into a journey of sonship. In his desperation he cried out to God, and he experienced the tangible love of the Father, time and time again. His wife moved out immediately, and his home became a constant reminder of his pain. Lesser men would have gotten out of that house as soon as possible. Not Mitch. He pressed into the darkness, inviting the Lord to meet him in the empty space.

The place of his greatest shame became a thinner space. His confidence as a beloved son positioned him to contend for a regular experience of God's tender presence.

Thinner spaces are more often uncomfortable. We feel the squeeze from certain external circumstances, or from our internal world, or from some combination.

The more we've established awareness of God's nearness, the less our circumstances will shake us.

Think of Jesus, napping in the boat in the middle of a storm. It was clearly a violent storm, yet, Jesus was undisturbed. His level of connection with the Father made Jesus not so easily ruffled.

When things shake us, it's an *opportunity* for us to more fully discover who God wants to be for us. It's not helpful to simply be annoyed at ourselves for being easily ruffled. The ruffling becomes a thinner space when we can acknowledge our pain, fear, grief, etc. and invite God to meet us there. Allow the pressure in your life to expose your lack of awareness of God's presence. Any space that causes you to ask things of God becomes a place of encounter.

God, as much as I don't want to admit it, I feel ________ about ___________. Please use this problem as an opportunity to show me who you are. What do you want to show me in this situation? Who do you want to be for me here?

CHAPTER 4
OFFENSE AND INSECURITY

I'VE BEEN RUFFLED A FEW TIMES. Well, actually...I am quite easily ruffled. In fact, I'm surprised I have any feathers left. It's incredibly humbling, when you're put in one of those high pressure spots and ugly ooze is what pours out of you. It's enough to make you want to run and hide!

It had been a few years since the days of third shift, and I was serving as a pastor of a small church in Urbana, Ohio. Everyone is called to ministry, but God had given me a specific call when I was reading Ephesians 4 in my early twenties. The words, "to equip the saints for the work of ministry" had jumped off the page. Even before I had a grid for God speaking to us personally, I heard the words spoken over my heart, "I'm not calling you to ministry, I'm calling you to equip others for ministry."

The pains of church leadership exposed my immaturities. Unlike other pastors I know, I really don't have sob stories of others mistreating me. I was ruffled by my own internal world. I was deeply insecure. No matter how many pats on the back I received for all my eloquence, I was sure they were saying different things behind my back. I felt like I was waiting for someone to stand up and expose me for a fraud. I didn't know what I was doing, and I was terrified of being found out.

Even scarier was the thought of what would happen next. That if people found out how incompetent I really was, they would leave me. To be honest, I wasn't so scared of a smaller attendance figure. No, I was afraid of being rejected and abandoned. I know how church works around here, if I come up short of what people want, they walk away. I counted people in my church as friends—and even family. The more connected I felt to them, the more terrified I was of them leaving.

My phone buzzed on the table in front of me. This was the awkward part of the Trustees meeting, where we looked at the numbers. I could see the various numbers were clearly less than the month before, and the month before that. Meanwhile the figure of my salary glowed off the page, an uncomfortably large fraction of the diminishing balance of the whole. I pulled my phone into my lap and took the opportunity to tune out for a moment. It was a text from Wes.

Wes had spent time in prison because he had fallen into a pattern of drug addiction that nearly devastated his family. But during his time in prison he had begun a deep work of healing. The first time I visited him was out of pastoral obligation. After that I returned several times. Wes was opening my eyes to what it looks like to pursue healing in partnership with the Holy Spirit.[1]

During his time in prison and after his release Wes and I became fast friends. We became companions on our parallel journeys of healing. We had a shared language, "the way of the heart".

1 Wes and I worked through the book *Waking the Dead* by John Eldridge. I highly recommend it.

We began to do recovery ministry together with others. At the same time, Wes had begun to create his own business and I would help him with jobs. Eventually I made space for him to be part-time on staff at church by becoming part-time myself. It was an exciting development, but tension quickly developed between us.

Holding my phone beneath the table, I read the text from Wes.

"Hey bro, turns out I'm not going to need you for the job tomorrow."

My face reddened. *How could he do this again? Doesn't he know I count on these handyman jobs?* The text, paired with the embarrassing facts of the Trustees meeting were like two pressure systems colliding, causing a whirlwind of emotion within me. I had to keep it together for the meeting. Under the table I lashed out at Wes through text.

"Are you serious, man? You know I'm counting on this work right?"

No answer.

"If I'm gonna do work for you, I need to know you'll stick to it."

No answer.

With every minute he didn't respond, I was getting more upset. I set it aside and gave my attention to the meeting. As I drove home, I realized that much of my frustration didn't belong to Wes. I was scared, and I was covering it with anger. I gave him a call. When he didn't pick up, I left him a voicemail. "Hey man, I'm sorry for my texts, I overreacted. I understand if things changed for tomorrow. Let's figure out when I can work for you next."

The angst continued through the night, into the next morning. Still no response from Wes. I was angry and hurt. It felt like Wes's fault. *He's the problem*. I was warned of his sudden relapses, maybe that's what's happening. I called his wife.

"Hello?"

"Hey Sara, it's Kyle."

"Hey Kyle, what's up?"

"Sorry to bother you, I just wanted to check on Wes. Is he okay?"

She was quiet for a minute. "As far as I know, why?"

"It's probably nothing, he's just not getting back to me. I just wanted to check with you and make sure he's not going off the deep end."

"Oh. No, I really don't think so. I think he's just busy."

I felt sick as I got off the phone. I had a sense I had done something wrong when I made that call. Months went by with almost no contact with Wes. He came to church less often, and when he did, he kept his distance. The pain of rejection was intense. I was an exposed nerve. That's when I started to become better acquainted with Offense.

I remember one of the many times Offense pulled into my driveway. His arm hung out the driver's window, muscular and covered in ink—monuments to his past. As he put the truck in park, he looked up at me. With his chin held high and his lips together and curved to one side, as if he were studying my mood.

"You look like you could use some bricks," he said.

Offense walked to the bed of his truck and opened the back. It was full of bricks and mortar, ready to mix. He always had plenty of bricks, and he loved to share. Sometimes the bricks were for building walls. He was an expert at building walls. He's built many walls for me, so high and so wide that I've never had to look at a person again. Other bricks were for throwing. These are smaller and made from lighter material.

"We don't want to kill anyone," he would say, "we just want them to get the message. They have disappointed us."

The throwing bricks have excellent questions engraved on them, like *Where were you?* And *Don't you even care?*

Offense taught me to measure my friends and family. Certain hurts should be punished, while others shouldn't be tolerated. When I would spend time with him, I would always feel better about myself. No...not better, superior. With him I could see the flaws of those around me so clearly, and I knew I was the better spouse, the better son, the better friend.

When my eyes would swell with tears from hurt, Offense reminded me, "You know, you don't have to feel pain. I can protect you. Let's think about who's at fault. When we know who to blame, we can focus our energy where we need it: retaliation and self-protection."

He taught me that going it alone is better. "Your 'friends' will fail you," he explained as he placed another brick on the wall, "so it's better you reject them before they reject you."

I used to feel so safe when I was with him. It seemed as though Offense had my back.

I can think of specific occasions where Offense was my companion. Once, I found myself in the corner of the room, under the stairs during a community worship event sitting with Offense. When I heard about the event I was initially excited. I'm all about unity in the Church. I believe each of our churches are positioned to bring the Kingdom to our community in a unique aspect, and when we seek to build the Kingdom more than our own institutions we'll see the Spirit flow among us and between us in a way we'll never see in our own silos.

But then Offense reminded me of the facts—as we saw them anyway. *If they're about unity, where were they? They haven't slaved in any prayer gatherings I've been a part of. I didn't see them step up in this or that event.* All of it felt so true! I found myself hoping hardly anyone would show up.

Boy was I disappointed when I showed up a few minutes late.

The lot was packed! I stepped inside and there was hardly room to walk through the back. Everyone looked too happy. I was sure they were faking it, but they were worshiping.

"Are they though?" Offense whispered as we found an empty spot in the back under the stairs. I wanted to worship, but Offense kept me pinned. I was bitter, resentful, and judging everyone up front.

Offense whispered comforting words, "You should be up there leading! But they stuck you in the back. They don't appreciate you."

Suddenly another friend whispered. I knew His voice immediately; it was the Holy Spirit.

"Kyle, this is exactly what you've prayed for. Why are you rejecting what I'm doing?"

In moments like this when the Lord's voice convicts my heart, it's amazing how good it feels. It's like removing a splinter. It stings, but there's immediate relief from the constant irritation that I had begun to accept. Hearing Him so clearly both crushed me and broke me free in a moment. It was like I had unknowingly been in bondage. A heavy yoke of resentment and bitterness had been choking the life out of me, then in a moment, it was exposed and I was free to step out from under it. I immediately apologized to the Lord and I prayed blessing over everyone up front.

Jesus, thank you for stirring all of our hearts to walk in unity with love and adoration for you. I celebrate my brothers and sisters and I bless what you are doing in and through them here.

My heart was flooded with love and honor for everyone in the room, and for the church hosting the event.

This wasn't the last of my conflicts with Offense. He still comes around with his bricks. But more often than not, I see his invitation for what it is and I send him down the road. The more secure we are in the love of God, the less appealing Offense's loyalty becomes. How often his appeal captures us in bitterness, resentment, competition, and hate. I find that when we let go of what we want someone to be for us, we are free to embrace who they really are.

I decided it was time to try again with Wes. It took a few tries, but I managed to get him to meet me for coffee. We sat on the back patio of The Depot, in the shade.

The Depot is exactly as it sounds. An old train station, remodeled as a coffee shop. The elegant curvature of the brick and the open interior, complete with large windows and original wood floors made The Depot a pleasant space for meetings and administrative work. I stopped holding office hours at the church because the space at The Depot was much more inspiring.

The back patio sat next to the train tracks, with a bike path alongside. On the other side of the tracks was a granary. The granary provided a constant low hum of active machinery. We managed smiles and small talk, but the tension was obvious.

I took a breath and started. "Look man, you've been avoiding me and it's really sucked."

"Yeah?"

His smile was unnerving. "Yeah. I consider you my friend, Wes. But I feel like you've just written me off. What did I do to deserve this?"

He tilted his head and raised an eyebrow. "Oh you want to talk about feeling hurt?" He raised his voice, "How about the time you called my wife to check on me?"

My throat tightened. "I called her because you wouldn't respond."

"Do you know how it feels, when your friend calls your wife, and assumes you've relapsed?" He stared at me intently. "Of course you don't. You don't know what it's like to feel like no one trusts you. It makes you start to question yourself. But I'm healthy man. I'm healthier than I've ever been. I thought you would know that better than most."

A knot formed in the pit of my stomach. I felt sick, and remorseful. "I'm sorry, Wes." My eyes began to well up. "I didn't think of how that would be for you. I was caught up in my own world. I'm so sorry."

Looking at the ground, he shook his head. "It's okay man, I forgive you."

We sat there in silence for a minute, not knowing where to go next. The tension was still there. Someone honked and Wes waved in their direction.

"I should go, I've got a lot to do. We good?"

"I guess." My heart stung. "I mean, you tell me."

"Yeah bro." He said with enthusiasm.

As he walked away I closed my eyes and let my head sink into my hands.

CHAPTER 5
ALONE IN THE WILDERNESS

"Let him who cannot be alone beware of community...
Let him who is not in community beware of being alone."
DIETRICH BONHOEFFER

IT WAS EARLY AFTERNOON when I pulled into the empty trailhead parking lot at the Red River Gorge. The only movement was from the colorful leaves falling around me. My chest felt tight, it took a lot of effort to breathe deeply. Normally the start of a hike was a celebratory moment, but this felt more like a funeral. The silence was uncomfortable. I had experienced that same silence in the car. I had wanted to turn around and head home for the entire drive.

This was supposed to be a trip for the four of us guys. We had planned it for months. Just a week before, the three of them canceled. They didn't say why, but I had heard about another trip that two of them planned to take together. Standing in the lot, by the trunk of my car, my jaw and fists were clenched. My chest tightened again. Every time I thought about it, my heart felt like it was in a vice grip. I wanted to scream. I wanted to cry.

The canceled plans were just a continuation of an increasing theme in my relationships with Wes and others. They had been distancing themselves from me for about two years. They would make excuses whenever they wouldn't show up.

"I'm just too busy right now."

It felt like a punch to the gut when I'd walk into The Depot and find them sitting together. *What the hell?* I'd do my best to smile and wave before I headed for the door. I'd get my coffee somewhere else.

When they first canceled, I had decided not to go. Just two days prior, I sensed the Lord's whisper, "I have something for you there."

The invitation didn't feel warm to me. It was another invitation to trust, and I was losing my nerve. The feeling persisted. I refused. Finally, someone who was not aware of the situation suggested I consider going for a hike alone. I was tempted to take offense, "Take a hike, pal!" But my sense of the Father's invitation was so strong that I couldn't deny it.

To be honest, I was following Melissa's example. For the last few years I watched her face places of deep pain from her childhood trauma. She showed me that sometimes the Lord invites us to face pain. She wasn't always graceful in the process, and some days she would avoid it. But more and more she would show up, allowing herself to feel anger, grief, and pain. She was real and raw, which allowed the Lord to meet her in the process.

It was an act of pure obedience when I opened the trunk and pulled out my pack. I had packed for two nights. The pain was so intense. There was no way I would last that long. I hoped the tightness in my chest would loosen once I started walking. It didn't. Every fiber of my being throbbed as I walked through the woods.

After hiking about a mile, I came to a stream crossing. I found a seat on a boulder next to the water. I sat in silence, listening to the water flow over the rocks. *Is it going to be like this the whole time?*

I would like a break from this pain. It was too cold to sit still for too long. I started moving uphill on the other side of the stream.

I tried praying. I prayed prayers of thankfulness, I sang worship songs, I invited Jesus to walk with me, pleading for him to let me feel his presence. None of these things alleviated the pain.

"You said you had something for me out here. What is it?" I was safe to talk out loud, I hadn't seen anyone on the trail. I raised my voice, "Why the f*** am I out here God?"

Now the pain was fully at the surface. My face was hot and my hands were clenched. "What the hell did I do to deserve this? I'm a good guy, right? Don't I love people well? Why do my friends always abandon me?"

A memory came flooding back to my mind. I was probably about eight years old, playing in my friend Rob's yard. Alex was with us. Rob and Alex were a grade ahead of me, so I was typically the odd one out. At that age, a year difference feels like a decade. "Oops!" Rob threw the ball over the wooden privacy fence.

"I'll get it!" I said.

I was always eager to impress with my speed and agility. I climbed the fence with ease and landed on the other side. The Wilson yard. The neighborhood kids called it "the jungle." Grass, weeds, vines, plants, all of it overgrown. Flower pots, unopened bags of soil, a broken wheelbarrow, and assorted trash littered the yard. I sorted through the jungle and found the ball. I tossed it over the fence and climbed over. Rob and Alex were nowhere to be found. I yelled for them. No answer.

What we experience in a moment as kids can have an odd sort of permanence. I felt panic rise up as I yelled for them, searching the front yard, down the alley and in the garage. I didn't think to ask why they disappeared, I just didn't want to be alone. I heard a noise from the back porch. I ran to the source. There, under a table, I saw the two of them snickering. In a moment I moved from panic to relief, relief to confusion, and finally, I flipped to rage. I ran home.

The grief of the memory pressed on me as I hiked. Other memories followed.

I stood for what felt like hours at my bedroom window, waiting for Nick to come down the street to play. He had just said on the phone that he was on his way. The longer I waited, the more furious I became. Finally, I gave myself over to the anger, punching the window. Glass shattered.

Fragments of any sense of security were lost in those moments, when I allowed the rejection of my peers to define my sense of worth.

I didn't have clarity on the mistakes I had made in these relationships, I just had raw pain. God wasn't reprimanding me; he was simply inviting me to face the pain. So I faced it. I told God exactly how I felt, not mincing my words. I held nothing back. I didn't care how accurate I was; I didn't try to defend my friends. I told the Father how they had hurt me. I told him how angry I was at him for allowing it to happen. He didn't correct me, but the more I expressed, the more I became aware that he was listening.

The Psalms give me a sense of permission to be so real and raw with God. David said some pretty nasty things, and yet God considers him a "man after his heart" (1 Samuel 13:14). If David has permission to be so real with God, so do I. In light of Jesus, I have even more access to the Father than David did. It seems as though no matter how ugly it gets; God considers the pouring out of my heart an act of worship.

A few stream crossings later, I found myself in a familiar spot on the trail. Unless it's an overlook, it's hard to tell particular spots on the trail apart. It all blends together when it's just trees on the side of a hill. Still, something seemed familiar about the incline I was hiking.

The intensity had begun to alleviate. Like an old wound that had been opened, the pressure of the fluid had drained, now the wound could heal. I began to release my friends from being what they were unable to be for me. *Jesus, I release Nick to you. I forgive him for not being what I needed, and I bless him to be who he is.* There was such relief in naming that reality: that they couldn't be for me what I wanted them to be. The weight lifted with each friend I named and released.

The Lord spoke to my heart, "I am the friend that's closer than a brother."

I knew that verse, I had memorized it as a kid, I was so drawn to it. "A man with many companions will come to ruin, but there is a friend that is closer than a brother," Proverbs 18:24.

When I had memorized it, I had heard it as wisdom; that it's better to have a few deep relationships than several that are shallow. I had never thought of Jesus as *that* friend. I felt his invitation to get what I've been longing for from friends, from him.

I continued up the mountain with gratitude and relief. So much weight had been lifted. Suddenly I remembered this stretch of trail. I had been here ten years before with my friends, Jeff and Luke.

It was our first backpacking trip together. We camped out at the top of this mountain, we called it Bernie Poo Point (It's better if you don't ask). When we arrived at the site, it was late in the day and we needed to hurry to set up before dark.

"You guys set up the tent and collect firewood, I'll go down to the stream to get water," I said.

It was this very trail I had excitedly hiked down toward the stream. I had always wondered what it would be like to be alone in the wilderness, and a little H_2O excursion would give me a taste of it. But as I descended it grew darker, and every noise felt like an alarm. The hair on my skin stood up on end. Here on this exact same stretch of trail I had said to myself, "I am never hiking alone."

Now here I was, alone.

I heard the Lord whisper, "Kyle, I want you to break that vow."

God had brought me back here, to remind me of a vow I had made over myself, "I refuse to be alone." God loves me enough to bring me to the very place of my pain so that He could tend to it, and so that I could learn to overcome it. The invitation to break the vow was an invitation to trust him, that there was some value in being alone.

I am never hiking alone. How often do we make a statement, oblivious to the weight attached to it? When God made humanity in His image, He gave us "dominion." He entrusted authority to us, because He always intended to partner with us. We still carry that authority. If we're not careful, we can use that authority in ways that cause damage, either to us or to others. We can make statements that may feel harmless, but we have the capacity to create worlds with our words. *This conversation is not going to go well. I can't fix this. He'll never amount to anything.* Such statements can become agreements we make with high costs.

Suddenly I became aware that my fear of being alone was costing me. I have not been comfortable in solitude and therefore I have avoided it. I couldn't see what value there could be in solitude, and I had unknowingly vowed to avoid being alone. Now God was inviting me to discover something good in solitude. I couldn't imagine anything good there, but I wanted to find out. Breaking the vow seemed to be a key. As I ascended the mountain,

I broke the vow.

"In Jesus's name, I break off my agreement with the fear of being alone. Father, you have gifts for me, hidden in solitude, and I refuse to miss them. I'm stepping—with my whole heart—into solitude."

Darkness was falling around me, but I was too light to notice. I think I danced the rest of the way up the trail.

At the top I found Bernie Poo Point. I began to set my gear down, then I noticed a faint path beyond camp. I followed it, through thick pines for about a hundred yards. It opened up and I found myself at a smaller campsite, a 270-degree overlook of the gorge.

As I enjoyed the view, I heard the Lord whisper, "There are places I'm taking you that you can only find when you're alone with me."

Sometime later, the Lord took me back to the memory of Rob's yard. I invited Jesus, "Show me where you were when this happened."

Sometimes when I do this, I'll re-experience the memory, this time with Jesus. It's amazing the ways he shows up. This time I climbed the fence into the jungle. I found the ball right away, because it was glowing. Fascinated, I picked it up. I stood there, holding the ball, my heart full of wonder. I climbed the fence with it. The boys were gone, hiding, but this time I didn't care.

My attention was no longer on them, or on their response to me, it was on the ball. It was radiant. I was completely content, alone in Rob's yard. I began walking in no particular direction, fixated on the beauty in my hands. I knew in my heart this ball was a picture of the Kingdom of God. It was the treasure hidden in the field, and it had my full attention. I heard him say, "Your motive for seeking me was not always pure, but you found me anyway. I belong to you, Kyle."

It's funny how the Lord knows our hearts, but he's not threatened by mixed motives. While I have sought the Lord, the seeking has often been intermingled with a desire for others to value and accept me. Still, I found Him. He showed me that my truest desire was for Him, and He does not disappoint.

He's given me a deep desire for community. I've never been interested in the life of a lone ranger, there's so much life in partnering with others. I know he loves that desire and he intends to fulfill it. But for now, he's teaching me to be alone with him; to find everything I need in him. I'm discovering that when we learn to be content in solitude, we can be trusted with community. As Leif Hetland says, "When you don't need it, then you can have it."[1]

1 *Called to Reign* by Leif Hetland—I have learned so much about being a beloved son from Leif Hetland. In fact, he's a primary influence on the next chapter.

CHAPTER 6
THE CURE FOR INSECURITY

THE DESIRE FOR COMMUNITY is good and right, it's the way God designed us. However, when we carry all of our unresolved needs into community, they are like a toxin, tainting the quality of our connections. Whenever we try to get our needs met in other people, there will be dysfunction and we will walk away disappointed.

In the book of Jeremiah, God confronts Israel for their dysfunction,

> For my people have committed two evils:
> They have forsaken me, the fountain of living waters,
> And hewed out cisterns for themselves,
> broken cisterns that hold no water.
>
> JEREMIAH 2:13

Israel had neglected to realize that their depth of need was meant to drive them to the fountain of living waters, and they sought out other sources. How often we approach other people in our lives for what we need. They become the material out of which we build broken cisterns. Often we don't even realize the depth of need we carry into our relationships.

I had my greatest breakthrough when my deepest fears were realized. When people rejected me, I was left alone with God. There was a constant ache that came with it, I couldn't deny the pain of solitude. I still didn't want to be alone, but I was determined to lean into it. God had things for me here and I resolved not to miss it.

I showed up to the cabin after dark. I used my phone as a flashlight, looking for a light-switch as I set my stuff down. The cabin was cold, just a few degrees higher than the air outside. I turned up the heat and made some tea. These occasional retreats were an opportunity to take a breath, a brief escape from the chaos of life. I would take a hike through the snow-covered woods that surrounded me. I'd worship, pray, and I'd study. But first, I'd enjoy a hot drink on a comfy chair in front of the fireplace.

I had noticed the fireplace the moment I stepped in. I wasn't excited to find that it was electric, but still, it could have nearly the same effect. I set my tea down on the table next to the chair and sat down. I dragged the chair as close to the fireplace as I could. The switch had three settings: *Heat, No Heat, and Off.* Why would anyone turn it on to *No Heat*? Who wants to look at fake flames when they're too warm for a fire? Unfortunately, when I selected the *Heat* setting, it was no different than the *No Heat* setting. I was stuck staring at a cold, fake fire.

I think for a lot of people, Christianity is stuck in the "no heat" setting. There's a lot of talk about the love of God, but little experience. Really, we're talking about affection. If you're going to tell me that you love me, you better be able to back it up. You can smother me with kisses, put your arm around me, bring me a gift, or share a meal with me.

Where there is love, there is meant to be an experience of that love: affection. Affection is most often thought of as loving touch, but more generally it's the act of affecting or being affected. It's the felt expression of love.

When we don't have an experience of something, it's hard to trust the reality of it. If I'm constantly telling my kids I love them, but I'm not expressing that in any way, they're going to become skeptical of that love. However, if affection is felt, with it comes a certainty that remains even in the moments that might otherwise feel uncertain. Affection is an experience that forms us.

The ministry of Jesus is the ministry of affection. He *is* the *expression* of the love of God. We see it all through Jesus's life. One of the clearest examples of this is the leper in Mark 1. As a leper, the man has been required to keep his distance from everyone in his community. Lepers are seen not only as threats, but as an embarrassment to their community. He has had such a deficit of affection, that while he doesn't question Jesus' ability to heal him, he's not so sure Jesus would want to.

> "A leper approached Jesus and knelt before him, 'If you're willing, you can make me clean.' Moved with compassion, Jesus stretched out his hand and touched him and said to him, 'I am willing. Be clean.' And immediately the leprosy left him."
>
> MARK 1:40-41

Look at the affection in Jesus' response. First, his heart is moved. Jesus sees the depth of this man's pain, and it stirs his heart. Second, Jesus touches the man. He certainly didn't have to touch him in order to heal him. How long has it been since this man has felt a touch from anyone?

Have you ever been surprised by how good a simple hand on

the shoulder felt? Apparently there is a hormone that is released in our body when we experience physical affection; oxytocin. Some call it the "cuddle hormone," I prefer to call it "*hugsytocin*." God wired us to need affection, because He intended to fill it.

Jesus comes filled to the brim with the expressed love of God, giving everyone the opportunity to find the fulfillment of deep longing. How? Not because he's God, but because he's a son; a beloved son. There is only one thing that enables Jesus to be such a display of God's affection for humanity. He is bursting with hugsytocin. The Gospel of John gives the most poetic and mysterious introduction to Jesus, and he ends the introduction with the most fascinating statement.

> No one has ever seen God; the only God (some manuscripts say, "the only Son"), who is at the Father's side, he has made him known.
>
> JOHN 1:18

If you look at the footnotes in your Bible here, you might find that in the Greek, the meaning of "*at the Father's side*" is "*in the bosom of the Father.*" John is secretly giving us the answer to the question Jesus is asked just a few verses later, "*Where do you live?*" (John 1:38).

Ultimately, Jesus's answer is, "*I live in the embrace of my Father.*"

Jesus's superpower is his intimate connection to the Father. He credits the Father for everything he says and does. Jesus's love and affection for others is an overflow of the love and affection of the Father.

Jesus doesn't approach people with one single unaddressed need. To be clear, Jesus does have needs, he is human after all. But Jesus regularly drinks from the fountain of living water. He receives everything He needs from the Father, which empowers Him to give freely to others.

This is the depth of security that I long for. I want to know the Father the way Jesus knows Him. And why not? Jesus himself says that He is the way to the Father (John 14:6). I have full access to the Father, and I plan to take full advantage.

I leaned back in my chair, ignoring the dancing flames of the fake fire in front of me. I closed my eyes. *Jesus, would you show me how to live in the embrace of the Father?*

I was standing beside a river. It wasn't deep, maybe waist high, and it was clear. Jesus was standing in the middle, looking at me with the brightest smile. He didn't say anything, He just laughed. Then He raised his arm toward me, and He motioned for me to join Him. I stepped out into the water. I was shocked to find that it was warm. The gentle sand greeted each step. I took my place next to Jesus, both of us facing upstream. He splashed me and laughed. I splashed Him back, He laughed harder.

He laid back into the water, letting himself sink to the bottom. I followed suit. As I sunk, I noticed that breathing wasn't an issue here. It was almost as if I had gills. Somehow I knew that I was made to live in this environment. You know how when you're underwater, you have a full-body sensation? It was like that, but magnified ten times. I could feel it over every fiber of my body, and with it there was a power surging through me. Somehow I was completely at rest, yet filled with might.

Jesus turned to me. "This is where I live." Whether He spoke out loud, or I heard it in my head, I don't know. "This is the Love of the Father, and I'm always immersed in it. I want you to live here with Me."

I opened my eyes, reacquainting myself with the dark room around me. My mug was empty and the room was still cold. I refreshed my mug with hot lemon tea and returned to my chair by the "fire." I grabbed my journal and began to write. I wanted to remember this experience.

Baptism is not simply a picture of death and resurrection, it's also a picture of immersion. The actual meaning of the word "baptize" is to "immerse." The nature of the thing that is immersed is changed. A pickle is a baptized cucumber. Where do we store the pickles? They live in the brine. Another translation for "baptize" is to be "overwhelmed." The cucumber is overwhelmed by its environment, and it becomes something else.

You and I are meant to live our lives immersed in the love of the Father. The highest aim of our lives is to position ourselves to more fully receive His Love. In John 13 He gives a new command, *Love one another as I have loved you (v. 34).* The greatest commandment of the old covenant is self-powered. "Love *with all your* heart, mind, strength." But the new command is empowered by something beyond ourselves. Our love is empowered by the love we receive.

The cabin never really got warm that night, and the fake fire didn't help. It sat there, mocking me. But I was experiencing a different warmth. Late into the night I read stories of encounters with the Love of God. Stories like John Wesley, who felt "waves of liquid love." And Charles Finney, who collapsed in surrender in the woods, and later felt the Love of God, flowing through him like electricity. Each story opened me up more and more to the move of God upon my heart.

The next morning, I looked out the window. The sun was out in full force, thawing the ground. The sound of melting snow and running water beckoned me to explore. I went for a walk. With each step I felt like my heart was going to burst. Every sight and sound was a gift from the Father, straight to me. I could sense His nearness, walking with me, watching the joy on my face with pleasure.

I began to tell Him how I felt.

"Father, you are everything I need. I don't need anyone else! You are the only One for me. I don't care if I ever do anything significant in my life! I just want to be with you. From now on, my only measure of success is that I would live in your love. My only goal is to stay in your love, to be your beloved son."

Insecurity is at the core of all that is wrong in my world, and I had found the cure: an immersion in the Father's love.

I stepped out of a wooded hillside, into an open field. I could hear the rush of a stream ahead. I walked through the field, looking down, taking note of the fleeting snow, exposing trampled grass. I stopped at the edge of the stream. I took in the scene around me, teeming with the life of spring beginning to peek through the fading winter.

I don't quite know how to explain what happened next, or why. I began to preach to the stream and the meadow…in an Irish accent. I proclaimed loudly of the love of the Father, that it was the cure of the world. I promised that love would not be held back, but that it would break through and set captives free.

I called forth an outpouring of the Holy Spirit—the expressed love of God—to pour over and fill that space with the knowledge of the heart of the Father. For at least fifteen minutes I declared the heart of God and promised redemption over that space.

I stopped suddenly and stood there in silence. I laughed at the absurdity of what I had just done. All the while I felt the power of what had just happened. *Creation waits with longing for sons of God to be revealed* (Romans 8:19). I am the fulfillment of that promise, and that space experienced its longing fulfilled.

CHAPTER 7

IMAGINATIVE ENCOUNTERS

The world is perishing for lack of the knowledge of God,
And the Church is famishing for want of His presence.
The instant cure for most of our religious ills
would be to enter His presence in spiritual experience,
to become suddenly aware that we are in God and that God is in us.
A.W. TOZER

ENCOUNTERS WITH GOD are essential to the Christian life. Transformation isn't the result of knowing facts or doing the right things. We were designed for encounters with God. Remember the Garden of Eden? It was the place of encountering and connecting with God. God's desire from the beginning has been for the whole earth to be filled with the knowledge of God. This is not an intellectual knowing, it's an experiential awareness of God.

He desires relationship with humanity, so much so that He appoints people to partner with Him in making Himself known. First Adam and Eve, then each generation after. He calls Israel His "Kingdom of Priests" (Exodus 19:6), and appoints them to carry His presence and blessing for the sake of the whole world. Jesus alone fulfills this appointment, then initiates an outpouring of God's Spirit, so that a life of encounters with God becomes available to us all.

When we encounter God—or have an experience in which we perceive His presence or activity, our emotions are engaged, and we become rooted and grounded in His affections. Simply put, encounters affect our hearts. A mustard seed is deposited, which eventually grows and expands to our thoughts, the way we relate and the way we behave.

God has hidden evidence of Himself everywhere we turn. Our senses become essential avenues that raise our awareness of God's presence, they are a built-in radar system. We can't see the wind, but we can see the effects of it. Listen to the rustle of leaves in the wind, how does that impact you? What happens to you when you smell lavender? Consider the experience of peeling an orange. Tune into the soft, bumpy skin. Juice sprays as you peel back the skin.

Every moment is filled to the brim with the potential to perceive something of God. Thomas Merton says it this way, "For just as the wind carries thousands of winged seeds so each moment brings with it germs of spiritual vitality that come to rest imperceptibly in the minds and wills of men."

Paul introduces a different sort of sense in Ephesians 1:18. The *eyes of the heart.* He prays that they would be *enlightened.* There is a sort of internal perception. I would argue that Paul is referring to the imagination. It's possibly the only sense capable of grasping the "riches of His glorious inheritance" (Ephesians 1:18). The imagination can take us further than our physical senses in comprehending the breadth, length, height, and depth of the love of Christ that surpasses knowledge (Ephesians 3:16-20).

I've been the recipient of the wonderful wisdom and resources of others while on the journey of learning to live in God's presence. I'd like to share what is perhaps the most important exercise I have ever come across. In fact, many of the stories I share come from this exercise. It's called "Safe Place."

Safe Place is an exercise where one releases past and future concerns, and is positioned—relaxed and receptive to the presence of the Lord through the use of the imagination. God loves to animate our imagination as a space for Him to reveal Himself to us.

Does the word "imagination" throw you? Does it cause something to be less real? Why do we have such a hard time trusting the imagination? The imagination is often discarded by the dominant worldviews of our culture as irrational and subjective. It's no wonder encounter with God is so absent in the western world!

We use our imagination all the time. In fact, anxiety is simply a hijacked imagination. Anxiety is nothing but the imaginings of negative outcomes. Just because those things sometimes do come true doesn't mean they didn't begin in the imagination. I believe the enemy of our souls has targeted our imaginations to keep us out of encounter. He has created such a mistrust of the imagination that we wouldn't poke it with a stick.

God often communicates visually. The Bible is full of visions, dreams, word pictures and analogies. The worldview of scripture doesn't seem to have a hard time with whether someone physically saw what was described. Peter sounds like such a hippie in Acts 10. He's sitting on a rooftop with the munchies, and he falls into a "trance." The word for trance here is *ekstasis*:

"a throwing of the mind out of its normal state...although he is awake, his mind is drawn off from all surrounding objects and wholly fixed on things divine that he sees nothing but the forms and images lying within"
(definition taken from Blueletterbible.com)

There is clearly an internal perception happening here. Peter is seeing with the eyes of his heart. What are the *eyes of your heart* if not the imagination? When we learn to see Jesus with the eyes of our hearts, we'll begin to see Him everywhere.

You might ask, "How do I know if it's God, or if I'm just making something up?" People ask me that all the time. We're so afraid of misrepresenting God that we'd rather not try at all. The same principle is true for prophecy and healing.[1] We're afraid that if we miss it, we'll do more harm than good. Don't get me wrong, there is a danger of being misled and we should be equipped to discern. But we're also in danger of putting more faith in our ability to be deceived than in the Holy Spirit's ability to lead us.

The Holy Spirit is quite capable of speaking to us. Often it's so hard to differentiate His voice from ours because He's inside of us!

If you're waiting to hear an audible voice from heaven, remember that God paid a price to put heaven inside of you. The greatest danger is not that you would get something wrong, but that you

1 When referring to "prophecy," I'm not talking about foretelling—although prophecy sometimes includes that. More generally, prophecy is perceiving God's speaking and sharing it with others for the purpose of building them up. See 1 Corinthians 14 for a further discussion on prophecy. As for "healing," I'll deal with that more in the next chapter. For the purpose of this chapter, I'm referring to moments in which we perceive that God wants to heal someone, so we partner with Him by sharing that and praying accordingly.

would harden your heart from hearing at all. Keep a humble posture, be willing to test what you hear and see, and you'll stay safe!

Here are a few questions you can ask, to make sure you are staying on track[2]:

1. Does it exalt Jesus?

One of the Holy Spirit's jobs is to magnify Jesus. If you are seeing/hearing something that causes Jesus to be bigger and more beautiful, chances are, you're probably onto something.

2. Does it contradict scripture?

If you think Jesus is telling you to lie to the police officer to get out of a ticket...you might want to read your Bible more. Seriously, learning to hear from God will motivate you to have a better handle on scripture!

3. Does it bear fruit?

Take note of what results in your heart and your life. Compare it to the fruit of the Spirit in Galatians 5:22-23. Does what you see/hear cause love, joy, peace, etc. to grow?

4. Do other believers confirm it?

We absolutely need community in order to grow in discerning God's voice in our lives. If you have an experience that you're not sure about, talk to someone who is further along in their journey with Jesus. Oftentimes we are interpreting our experiences with some blind spots, and others can help us to see them.

5. Does it come to pass?

It's much easier to tell if something was God in hindsight. That's okay! Be willing to make mistakes and commit to looking back at the

---

2 I learned these questions from Adventures in Mission.

things you thought were God. This is what we call a feedback loop, which is necessary for our growth. As you look back, can you tell what was your voice and what was God? Can you see how assumptions caused you to misinterpret what God was saying?

SAFE PLACE PROCESS[3]

If you are currently not in a private place or time in which you can engage fully with this process, set it aside and come back later. Plan to give it about ten to fifteen minutes. This process is only as helpful as your ability to be present.

- Sit quietly in a comfortable position.
- Take several deep breaths, letting them out slowly. Take your time here, don't move on until you feel your body start to relax.
- Begin to whisper your feelings to God. If you're anxious, tell Him. Tell Him how you feel about Him. Offer Him thanks for who He is to you.
- After a few moments, invite the Holy Spirit to use your imagination to lead you to Jesus.
- Ask the Spirit to create within your mind a safe place where you can meet the Lord. It may be an imaginary place or somewhere you have been before that is special, like a cabin, beach, or spot along a quiet stream. You might feel like you supplied the place rather than the Spirit, but that's okay. Jesus doesn't mind if you choose the place, He just wants to meet with you.

3 I learned Safe Place through the ministry of Healing Care, https://www.healingcare.org/

- Rest there for as long as you like, enjoying all the surroundings. If you experience some dissonance or distraction, notice it and let it pass, like a leaf in the stream.
- When ready, invite the Lord to join you in that place. If that frightens you, ask Him to come as the lamb, or to simply allow you to feel His presence.
- Once there, notice the warmth of His love. Let it soak into your being. If you are allowing Christ to be there, notice His posture, eyes, and extended arms. Draw close to Him if you desire.
- When ready, tell Jesus how you feel about Him. Ask how He feels about you. He may respond with words or maybe actions. Either way, experience His acceptance and delight.
- If you are ready to conclude the exercise, simply spend a few moments in thanks and praise.
- Take a few deep breaths, letting them out slowly.

If you just attempted this, I am giving you a standing ovation! I want to encourage you that for many this is a hard process to lead yourself through. Don't be discouraged if you had less than satisfactory results. It may take practice and you might need help. If you have a desire for encounter and you are acting on that desire, God made you a promise.

> "You will seek me and find me,
> when you seek me with all of your heart.
> I will be found by you, declares the Lord."
> JEREMIAH 29:13-14

I want to pray a blessing over you...

Father, I thank You that your desire to meet with this reader is even greater than their desire for you. Before the foundation of the world, You had an intense desire to walk with this person. Thank You that you are closer right now than they realize. I take authority on their behalf, and I command that any unknown resistance in their heart and mind be exposed and broken. I bless them with the Spirit of Revelation. I speak to the eyes of their heart, their imagination, be opened to the Presence of God.

CHAPTER 8

DOWNLOADS AND HIGHLIGHTS

I WILL NEVER STOP being fascinated by the experience of walking in the Spirit. Encounters with God have a way of oozing out of our hidden life and into our everyday lives. Encounters position us for adventure in the midst of normalcy.

A friend told me the other day that she had lost her measuring tape. As she walked around the house, she almost absent-mindedly asked, "Lord, where did it go?" Right away a picture came to her mind and she ran to the linen closet. There she found what she was looking for in an obscure corner of an obscure closet—exactly as she pictured it. I hear stories like this all the time now. The Holy Spirit seems to specialize in finding lost things.

When Melissa and I came to Urbana, we were almost immediately pulled into SoKM (School of Kingdom Ministry). The goal of SoKM is to train people to walk with the Spirit in their everyday lives, and to partner with the supernatural activity of the Kingdom of God. I was drawn to the school when I heard its origin story.

Putty Putman was well on his way toward a career in physics when he began attending a local church. He sat in the back with his arms crossed as leaders claimed to have words of knowledge (specific information given to them by the Holy Spirit) and prayed for physical healing. For years he scoffed at their claims from a safe distance, until he found himself smack dab in the middle of an undeniable healing.

After that moment Putty shifted course and began using skills and systems from the physics world to understand and communicate the Kingdom of God. He also had experience instructing karate, so he developed practices that helped people build muscles and skills around tuning into the Spirit and taking risks. Melissa and I facilitated Putty's school for years, mostly because it gave us a space to step into what we call a *naturally supernatural* lifestyle.

When we give ourselves over to a lifestyle of walking with God, we can rest assured that we will be frequently invited into adventure and risk taking. It can't stay simply an experience just between us and the Lord, because the Lord has such an intense love for people. He invites us to partner with Him in expressing His heart to the people around us. This is often risky because it makes us vulnerable to the people we approach. People have the God-given capacity to reject love, and negative experiences have caused people to be guarded.

While hurrying to my next meeting, I passed a woman walking on the side of the road a few miles south of town. *Turn around and offer her a ride.* I had heard a voice in my mind like that before. It always seemed to come when I was running late! I shook it off. Then I heard it again, *Go back and offer her a ride.* I gave a dramatic sigh, making sure He knew I was irritated, and turned around.

Walking northbound with a faded rain jacket and wearing too much makeup, she looked to be in her mid-fifties. "Ma'am, do you need a ride?" I asked.

Eyes wide, she looked at me for a moment, then climbed in the passenger seat. We made small talk as we approached town.

I prayed silently. *What are you wanting to do? You're the one who wanted to pick her up.* I was looking for a download; some kind of direction, or something the Lord might want to do for this person.

I didn't sense Him saying anything in response, but I felt a tingling in my left ear. "This might sound odd, but do you by chance have any issues with your left ear?"

She shot me a look. "I can't hear anything out of that ear, why?"

I was as surprised as she was. "Seriously? How long has it been that way?"

"It's been about twenty years since I could hear out of it. My boyfriend at the time hit me on that side of the head, and I haven't heard since. How did you know that?"

"Sometimes God will give me a sense that someone needs healing. He does that because He wants to heal someone and show them that He loves them. I believe that God wants to heal your ear right now. Would you like that?"

Her lip began to quiver. She nodded. I pulled over at a gas station.

"Is it ok if I put my hand on your ear?"

Tears were starting to form. She nodded again.

I put my hand on her ear. "Jesus, we invite you to come now and make yourself real to Brenda."

We waited in silence for a moment. She took a few deep breaths as tension eased from her shoulders. I asked, "Are you experiencing anything?"

"Yea, peace—" Her head shot up, "I can hear you! Oh my God! Oh my God!"

"No way! Plug your right ear and I'll whisper. Tell me if you can hear me."

She plugged her right ear.

Quietly I whispered, "Jesus loves you."

She leaned forward, putting her head in her hands as she cried.

"Jesus loves you Brenda. He healed you because He wanted you to experience His love for you. And that peace you felt, that was Him. You can have that peace for the rest of your life. Would you like that?"

She nodded.

Downloads are seeds, dropped to us from God in a moment. God is entrusting something of the substance of heaven to us for the sake of the world around us. Sometimes a download comes subtly. It can come as a slight sensation, somewhere in our body, as a clue of something God wants to do for someone. If we're not sensitive, the sensation will leave as quickly as it came. But, if we learn to pay attention, and we're willing to make a few mistakes, we'll see heaven come before our eyes.

Sometimes they're not so subtle. One time in SoKM we were practicing hearing things from the Spirit to share with people in public. The goal was not to weaponize religion, or to "get 'em to church," but to get a download from heaven that would give them a taste of God's heart for them. After spending time soaking in God's presence, we wrote down things we heard, then we headed to the grocery store. We walked around the store in pairs, asking God to show us who our words were for. We each shared with someone. People left interactions with us beaming.

Heading for the door, I joined Ryan, who kept his head down. "Did you get to share with anyone Ryan?"

"I couldn't find anyone that I felt it was for."

I was determined to help him take a risk. "Come on, I bet they're this way." I led him to the produce aisle. I pointed to a middle aged man examining the cauliflower. "Is that the guy?"

"No." Ryan turned around, and stopped one aisle over. Halfway down the beer aisle was a young guy wearing sunglasses with long dark hair and a longer beard. His forearms were tense and covered in ink, carrying a sixteen-ounce Natural Light in each hand. *Oh boy.* He started walking toward us, a hard expression on his face.

"That's the guy."

"Hey man, how's it going?" I half smiled at him. He stopped about five feet short of us, looking at me, waiting. "I'm Kyle, and this is my friend Ryan. He has something encouraging he wants to share with you."

The man stood still, waiting. Ryan gave a big sigh. He looked down at his paper and began to read. I watched the man's face as Ryan read. At first he was completely unchanged. Then Ryan said, "I feel like God showed me that you have been longing for truth. You've searched for it in a variety of places and you've been disappointed in your search." The man's eyes widened and Ryan continued. "God sees your heart and He sees your search as noble. It pleases His heart to see you searching so diligently."

The shift in his face was so subtle, until the tears began to form. He set his cans down on the pallet of beer beside him and wiped his eyes.

"How the hell did you know that about me? Do I know you?" I honestly couldn't tell if he was about to hit us or hug us.

"No man, this isn't us. This is God. God showed me this about you, because He knows who you are." Ryan was no longer looking down. He continued, "You've been searching for truth and God wants you to know, you'll find what you were looking for in Jesus."

A rich discussion on the search for truth ensued at the end of the beer aisle, and it continued for two years before Ryan led him to receive Christ.

For the Spirit searches everything, even the depths of God. For who knows a person's thoughts except the spirit of that person, which is in him? So also no one comprehends the thoughts of God except the Spirit of God. Now we have received not the spirit of the world, but the Spirit who is from God, that we might understand the things freely given us by God...We have the mind of Christ."

1 Corinthians 2:10-16

Downloads are insights God gives us into the situations and hearts of those around us. He shows us things about people that we wouldn't otherwise know, because it gives God a point of access to reveal himself personally to them. Jesus modeled for us what it looks like to access this kind of insight when he met the woman at the well. In the heat of the day, Jesus shared a download he received from the Father, "You are right in saying, 'I have no husband'; for you have had five husbands, and the one you now have is not your husband. What you have said is true." (John 4:18) Suddenly, God gets our attention.

Then there are highlights. Someone or something stands out to us. Do you ever catch yourself staring at someone and you don't know why? For some reason, people are consistently highlighted for me at the market just a few blocks from my house. I honestly don't shop there often, but when I do, someone usually stands out to me. It's like they catch my eye. When it happens, I've learned to ask the Spirit, "Is that you?" Sometimes it's clear, other times it's not.

Once again, I was running late for a meeting. I was driving past the market and I noticed a woman my age walking the opposite direction, towards the market. My attention was drawn to her and I felt the strong urge to go and talk to her. I pushed the feeling aside, resolved to get to my meeting, which happened to be a block away. As I parked I began to feel tense and my body was getting warmer and warmer. As the intensity increased I knew God was making himself clear.

Everything in me wanted to ignore it, but the thought popped into my head, *My relationship with you is more important than convenience or being prompt.*

It was as though some more mature part of me was offering up a prayer and inviting the rest of me to agree.

I headed toward the market on foot. I thought maybe I had missed her, but as I entered the store, she was headed out. I had no clue what to say to her. But as our eyes met, it was clear that she had been crying. Without thinking, I said, "It's not too late, there's hope."

She couldn't contain the grief. As she sobbed, I put my hand on her shoulder and prayers flowed from my heart. God's presence began to fill the entryway of the market.

As she regained control, she explained that she had just come from court, and that she was close to losing custody of her kids. "I know what I need to do. I want to change my life, I really do! But it's so hard."

Compassion welled up within me and words began spilling out. "Right now, God is telling you that it's not too late, you still have time! He believes in you. But you're not going to be able to make the changes you need without His peace. Do you know Jesus?"

"Yeah, I used to go to church." Her eyes began to glaze over. "I should go back."

"It wouldn't be a bad idea to get around a community who can walk with you, but I'm not asking about church. Jesus himself wants to walk with you in this, and you need His peace. Do you want to receive Jesus in your heart?

A wave of calm came over her, she took a deep breath and nodded her agreement.

God often highlights people and places to us because He wants to invite us into where He's already working. Contrary to popular belief, God doesn't prefer to work alone. He loves to show us what He's doing and invite us into it. It's one of His many love languages. "For the Father loves the Son and shows him all that He Himself is doing." (John 5:20). Jesus isn't just flaunting His access to the Father here, He's paving the way for you and I.

Like downloads, highlights are most often subtle. If we're not paying attention, we'll disregard it and move on. The more tuned in to the reality that the Spirit is with us, the more we'll notice when people and places are being highlighted.

Sometimes we are the one that's highlighted to other people. Have you ever caught someone staring at you? When it happens, you might want to check for any loose boogers or downed zippers. If you're good there and they're still staring, it's possible that they are drawn to the Holy Spirit in you and they don't even know it!

I was meeting with a friend for coffee at The Depot, and this guy seemed to be staring right at me. I looked behind me to make sure it wasn't someone else, I made sure I didn't have anything out of place (No boogies? Check. Zipper? Check.). I even stared at him for a moment to make him aware that he kept staring! I tried so hard to ignore him that I don't think I heard much of what my friend said. After about thirty minutes of this, I couldn't take it. I'm not afraid of confrontation, I'd just ask him about it.

He watched me walk toward him, his hand holding a smoothie on the table in front of him. He was a block of muscle, he looked to be about twice my size. As I walked toward him, it occurred to me, *God's doing something here.* I started to imagine that this guy was drawn to the Spirit in me, I pictured a neon sign over my head. Now I was getting excited. God was gonna show up for this guy and I'd get to be a part of it! I hadn't a clue what was happening or what to do.

"Hi!"

Confused, he responded, "Um, hi."

"I noticed you looking at me, do we know each other?"

"Oh, I wasn't looking at you." His face was flat.

I thought to myself, *Yea right you weren't.* I stood there awkwardly for a moment.

I wish I could say that every time the Lord gave me something to share with a stranger, I immediately knew what I was going to say before I approached them. More often, the Lord directs me to approach someone and I don't know what I'm going to say until I begin to engage with them. I have to be willing to create an awkward moment, hoping God will fill it. This time He did.

At that moment, God gave me a picture. "Can I share something encouraging with you?"

This is a typical way I share something God gives me for someone I don't know, because it's disarming. Plus, I really believe that if God is giving me something to share with a stranger, it's probably going to be encouraging. He's not going to ask me to tell a stranger that He wants them to move to Germany. At least, I hope he won't...

"Sure."

"God gave me a picture of you just now. Uh...you were banging your head against a brick wall hopelessly. You took a few steps back, you took a breath, then you ran head-first and the wall fell away and you were able to move forward."

I was nervous. I had no clue whether this had meaning for him. "I feel like you are facing a hopeless situation, and God wants you to know that He sees you and He's with you. He wants to encourage you, you will get through this."

He remained expressionless the whole time. He said, "Thanks," and took a sip of his smoothie, then he resumed his staring in another direction. I walked back to my friend and continued our conversation. I sat there wondering if any of that was Spirit-led, or if I had made it up.

About a week later, I was running through my neighborhood. I had agreed to dog-sit for a friend, and the dog had gotten loose. Muscle Man happened to be out walking, and I asked him if he'd seen the dog.

"No," he responded as he took a closer look at me. "Hey, do you remember me, from The Depot?"

I laughed, "Yeah, I remember."

"I've been thinking about what you said." He stood silently for a moment, his face as flat as our last conversation. "My wife has stage four cancer. She's dying. It's been going on for about two years now." He paused again. "I think it's that brick wall you were talking about."

I wish I could say that God highlighted me to Russell so that I could go and pray for his wife, and she would be healed. It didn't play out that way. She died shortly after that initial conversation. Instead, that was the beginning of a friendship. It turned out Russell was a retired prison guard with a black belt. That explains the flat expression. I'm so glad I didn't pick a fight.

Russell and I would meet for lunch, and eventually he would open up about his fear of being alone. God had me on assignment to walk with Russell through that transition, and the picture He gave me accelerated the trust process, because Russell needed a friend. I was able to represent the heart of the Father to Russell in a vulnerable season, all because God had put a neon sign above my head and I was willing to take a sloppy risk.

Walking with God leads us into risk, and risk carries the potential to drive us nearer still. Risk requires trust and trust is cultivated in places of increasing risk. Nobody likes to be uncomfortable, but hunger for more of the Lord's presence has a way of overcoming our propensity for comfort.

CHAPTER 9

BEAR THE YOKE

THE HIGHWAY WAS FAIRLY OPEN on this particular sunny day in July. There wasn't much traffic this far from the city. We had been on the road for four hours, with several more to go.

To my left, the wide median was rolling with green hills and sparse trees, the southbound lanes lay on the other side. To my right, Melissa was reclining in the passenger seat, reading a novel. The kids each had headphones, watching a movie.

I daydreamed of what it would be like to work on the maintenance crew of the resort we left behind that morning. I was seriously considering turning around and asking if they needed one more for their crew. We'd just spent a week at the beach, sharing a house with friends. It truly was a magical experience, but that's not what inspired my daydream. I did not want to go back to our current life.

There were too many problems in the church that I didn't know how to resolve. The things I wanted to try didn't fit with the rest of the leadership. For years I had always stood in the tension, between those who wanted to make big changes, and those who wanted to move slow and steady. For the past year, the former group seemed to be making a gradual exodus from the church.

Just a few months into the pandemic, it all came to a head. We had stopped meeting in person like many churches, and many of us could sense the opportunity to do church differently. Melissa and I felt that we had an opportunity to experiment with our gathering format. Since it was recommended not to have large gatherings, what if we coordinated house groups? We could do a portion of the gathering together on zoom, but then entrust much of the elements of service to each individual house group.

It seemed like a chance to explore models of church that were less dependent on all of the centralized elements: professional leaders, polished sermons, and coordinated plans could take the back seat for a minute. Smaller groups could discern faithfulness together through their own expressions. We could learn to share responsibility and power to pursue God together, all the while finding creative ways to stay connected to one another.

Just a month before our trip to the beach, we pitched the idea to our leadership team. We were surprised to find that the team did not share our enthusiasm about the opportunity. They loved the current experience of our gatherings and only wanted to discuss how to move toward normal.

Melissa and I found ourselves grieved by their response. Experimenting with the expression of church seemed like exactly where the Lord was leading us. Maybe it was, but that wasn't shared by others. Not long after that decision, others in our fellowship who shared that conviction began to walk away. We could no longer toe the line between those who wanted change and those who brought stability.

To be honest, I hadn't a clue what the "right thing to do" was. I had severe decision fatigue.

I'm much more comfortable supporting someone else's leadership. I make a great sidekick! I've asked the Lord countless times,

"Why am I here? Why do you have me in this position? *Did* you put me here, or was this a mistake?" No, I knew He had called me here, it was undeniably clear. So then, *why?*

About a year ago I heard clearly from Him when I asked for permission to step away from leadership. I had written in my journal, "Lord, I'm so tired of leadership. I love ministry, I'm not tired of that. But is there any way I can walk away from leadership in the church? I would be happy to do handyman work and have more freedom in ministry."

Often when I express my heart to the Lord in writing, I'm more connected to the conversation. When I ask questions in writing, sometimes I can sense His responding and I carry on the back-and-forth in writing. He responded, "Sure, you can do that, if you want to. But it's not what I'm asking you to do. I'm calling you to be a midwife for the Church."

I didn't know what that meant, but it sounded gross. I don't do well with blood. When my daughter was born, they handed me the scissors to cut the umbilical cord.

Melissa took one look at me and said, "Give them back the scissors! You're white as a ghost!"

She wasn't wrong, I nearly passed out. I was trying to keep it together for the moment, but for some reason Melissa didn't want me near our child with scissors.

A midwife for the Church? Sounds like a big deal. God tends to speak to us about our destiny as though we're much more important than we realize. One of us is going to have to adjust our expectations...

In moments of pain and disappointment, it feels like I am a virus, causing destruction and damage in the church. Everything in me wants to get out and get away before I'm found out. I imagine someone connecting the dots and realizing, "It all comes back to that guy!" But no one ever does. While He had given me permission to walk away, I knew I couldn't. For reasons beyond my comprehension, God had me on an assignment.

Alone with my thoughts, driving down the highway, I recognized that I was falling into escapism again. It was time for a little game I like to call, *The Five Questions.*[1]

What am I feeling?

I'm feeling scared, slight panic. A bit stressed. Definitely helpless.

What happened?

Vacation is over. I have to step back into the same cruddy situation that I don't know how to resolve. I have no sense of direction. I feel trapped. My friends have left. I can sense others are on the verge of leaving. I'm thinking of getting "failure" tattooed on my forehead.

How am I tempted to cope?

Run away! That doesn't seem realistic, so I'll settle for going numb. I'll check my phone every other minute. I'll anesthetize the pain with distraction.

What Core Longing is absent and in need of care? (Love, Security, Belonging, Understanding, Purpose, Significance?)

Security. People are walking away on a regular basis. With each loss comes a weakening sense of safety or wellbeing. My house is made of sand.

---

1 The "Five Questions" is another tool I've picked up from the Healing Care community

What lies are you believing?

Too many to count. 1) My value is determined by others. 2) My wellbeing is dependent on how others respond to me. 3) I am a failure. 4) Everyone will leave me eventually. 5) The conditions around me are all my fault. 6) I am being punished.

The sun began to go down as we navigated the mountains of West Virginia. I could feel fatigue setting in, and the gas tank was low. We exited the highway and found a cheap motel for the night. After the kids were settled into bed, Melissa headed for the shower. I laid in the bed and returned to my thoughts.

Okay Jesus, these things feel true, but I know they aren't. I repent of believing these lies. I reject these lies. Holy Spirit, show me what's true. I took a deep breath and let my body sink deeper into the bed beneath me. I closed my eyes, anticipating that the Lord would give me a picture.

I saw myself in space, in a space suit, just outside of a ship. I was holding onto the ship, aware that if I let go, I'd be totally disconnected from anything. I would free float into oblivion. An accurate picture for what I was feeling.

Jesus's voice broke in, "Let go."

I let go. I could feel the sheer panic as I slowly moved out of reach of the ship. I was too far to even kick off. The panic was intense, and familiar.

I took a breath. "Okay Jesus, I know you're here. Show me where you are."

I waited, floating further and further from the ship. Then I noticed something for the first time. I was wearing a jetpack. Just one button and I could be propelled in any direction. I could head back toward the ship, or I could go off, further into the deep!

Jesus explained, "I am your secure base. I am your only fixed point. Everything and everyone else in your life can come nearer or move further away at any point. They can be taken away, they can leave you behind. I cannot and I will not. Because of my covenant with you, I am as near to you as I ever will be, and I will never be further."

Upon returning home, I reached out to my counselor to schedule our next appointment. There was more to process here. When something is at the surface, you don't want to waste an opportunity. The temptation is always to avoid pain. We are a highly pain intolerant culture. We push pills like nobody's business. I'm not anti-medicine. But when we make pain our enemy, we're destined to go in circles. We'll never face the things that are at the root if we're always cutting the weed at the surface.

Pain is rarely the problem, but pain will lead you to the source of the problem. The fear of pain, however, leads to deeper problems. Some friends and I love to say, "I am a Giant Killer. I run toward my giants!" We can face pain with courage, because we know that the goodness of God is bigger than any problem.

Every negative emotion carries for me an opportunity to discover a new layer of the goodness of God. Emotional pain draws my attention to deep wounds and lies I'm believing that need to be addressed. Sometimes these things do deserve my attention, but they never have to derail me. I can still be who I am, and live from that reality, despite how I feel in the moment. I can still worship in the midst of pain. I can love. I can rest in the firm reality that I am dearly loved, even while the pain is intense.

My emotions are a gift and an asset, they are not a curse or a weakness. God doesn't judge me for my negative emotional responses. Instead, He embraces me in the midst of them. He sees them as an opportunity for Him as well.

I poured out my heart to my counselor. I explained the sense of panic and despair as I drove home from vacation. I explained the desire for permission to run away from my current circumstance. She waited quietly when I stopped. She had a tendency to draw more out of me by simply being comfortable with silence. Many times in these moments I would go through spurts of pouring out anger, confusion, hurt, grief about my present circumstance while she waited patiently. This time I let out a sigh and closed my eyes.

"What is it that you want right now?"

Before I could consider the question I answered, "I want to be free. I was made for adventure and discovery, and I feel restricted."

The weight of restriction suddenly felt real. I closed my eyes as she created space with her silence. I imagined weights being placed on me, like an athlete in training. I became aware of Jesus, standing before me. We were on the trail, next to an overlook. He was facing away from me, with his hands behind his back, looking out over a valley. He was wearing a black t-shirt and khaki hiking pants. I'm tempted to question when I see Jesus wearing what I would wear, *Am I making Jesus in my image?* No. The truth is that He and I are one, my clothes fit him. He likes to wear what I wear, and I look like Him.

I wanted to stand next to him, to look out and see what he saw. But I was glued to my spot, about ten yards behind him. It was darker where I stood, the air wasn't clear; it was thicker, like a fog. Without turning to face me, he spoke. "I am the one who put restraints on you. I'm training you, so that you can handle more freedom. I made you for adventure and discovery, Kyle. You have more limitations now so that you can have less in the long run."

I spoke out loud what I heard Jesus saying. I asked my counselor, "Does that sound like Jesus?"

"Do *you* think it sounds like Jesus?"

I groaned as I tilted my head. "I'm only hesitant because I don't like the thought of Him restricting me. But it does sound like Him."

"Interesting. The verse I keep hearing is Lamentations 3:27, it is good for a man that he bear the yoke in his youth."

I grabbed my Bible. I was familiar with Lamentations 3, but I had never heard that verse. Sure enough, there it was, on the heels of a familiar passage,

The Lord is good to those who wait for him, to the soul who seeks him.
It is good that one should wait quietly for the salvation of the Lord.
It is good for a man that he bear the yoke in his youth.
Let him sit alone in silence when it is laid on him.

"That sounds like Jesus to me," my counselor broke in. "God disciplines us because he loves us. He's invested in your development more than your comfort. He's confident in your ability to handle it, he trusts you. He's going to move you in such a way that he can entrust more to you."

I sat across from my counselor, shaking my head. I felt like I had just been given a new set of glasses. *I'm in training. The things I'm facing are a gift, meant to strengthen me to handle more of what I long for. Jesus wants to entrust me with more freedom, he wants to position me for more adventure and discovery! It's important that I take my training seriously. I don't want to waste it!*

There are circumstances we need to be delivered from, then there are circumstances we need to be strengthened for. God absolutely wants to be our deliverer, but he also wants to empower. Psalm 18 captures this contrast well. In the first half of the Psalm, the writer is crying out for rescue, and God is responding, "From his temple he heard my cry...He bowed the heavens and came down... He rescued me from my strong enemy." (vv. 6-19)

Then the scene switches and the writer is now a powerful warrior. He runs against a troop and leaps over a wall. "God equips me with strength" and "trains my hands for war." Ultimately the psalmist-turned-warrior beats his enemies fine as dust. In Psalm 18, God moves from deliverer and warrior to trainer and empowerer. The writer shifts from helpless to powerful.

There are seasons in our life when God allows a heavy yoke to be placed upon us. If we run from it, we'll miss what God is doing in us and we'll lack the strength required for the battles ahead. If, however, we can learn to embrace these seasons with God, we'll discover a strength that was previously unimaginable.

CHAPTER 10

EMBRACE THE ACCLIMATION

NOT LONG AFTER meeting with my counselor, Mitch called. Mitch had been living alone for the last few years since his wife left. It's been such a beautiful privilege to walk alongside him through the process. Some days were dark and painful, but he remained diligent to receive everything he needed from the Father.

He had been learning to roast coffee from an expert, and he wanted to take me to the roaster and show off what he was learning. He picked me up and we headed for the city. We talked and laughed as we drove through the countryside. The sun streamed in my window as I watched the fields passing by.

"So I got another promotion with Honda." He said in a matter-of-fact tone.

After everything blew up with his wife, he left his job at the coffee shop. He needed some distance from everything in order to heal. He started working for Honda a year ago, and already he was quickly moving up the ladder.

"Again?! It's only been two months since the last one!"

"I'm already up three dollars an hour from when I first started, and I'm getting more vacation days now."

"Not even fair, dude. I've been in my job for over five years, and I'm getting less than when I started." I raised my eyebrows. "Is it wrong for me to want a promotion? I can't even imagine a scenario where that would happen."

"Have you ever asked the Lord?"

"Not really."

He laughed. "Why don't you ask God to give you a promotion? I'm sure He wants to give you one, and it can look any number of ways. He's probably just waiting for you to ask." After a pause, Mitch said a prayer. "God, I know that you love Kyle, and that you want to give him a promotion. Would you open up space in Kyle's heart to trust that and to receive it?"

The idea of asking the Lord for a promotion was new to me. I sat with the desire for the next few weeks, giving it permission in my heart.

Dad and I sat on the edge of the rocky cliff next to the water. With our feet hanging in the cold water, we began to put our gear on.

My dad is obsessed with being in water. My fondest memories as a kid were at the hotel pools. Dad became something else when he was submerged. He would torpedo from one end to the other, then walk on his hands back to the shallow end. He would float with his back facing up and my brother and I would pretend he was a boat dock. We'd see how many times we could jump off his back before he came up for air. Sometimes we couldn't believe how long he'd stay under. We'd try to pull him up, convinced that he needed a breath.

After getting our masks, snorkels and fins on, we hopped into the water. We came to the rock quarry, to warm up with some snorkeling, in hopes of preparing for a scuba diving trip in the future.

The cold took our breath away. I peeked under water, a dark forest of seaweed loomed beneath our feet. I'm not sure if my teeth chattered from the cold or from my imaginings of what lurked in the dark.

Dad took the first dive. I watched him as he swam to about ten feet below the surface. He paused, blowing air in intervals. Then he came back up to the surface, cleared his snorkel, and took a few breaths before diving to ten feet again. I watched him as he did this several times. He had explained to me, "At about eight to ten feet below, there is a change in pressure. Your body has to learn to acclimate at this level, before going deeper. If your ears pop when you blow air out, you're ready to go further. If you can't get them to pop, you have to come back up for air before you try again."

Once I mustered up the courage to dive into the weeds, I played around with it. A few times I was able to get my ears to pop and venture further into the darkness. About twenty feet down, you can feel an instant temperature change. It gets even colder!

A week after our dive, I found a spot in the back corner of The Depot. I sit in this corner when I don't want to be interrupted. A short wall juts out, creating a little cove. I put my headphones in, put on instrumental music, and invited the Spirit to speak to me. I closed my eyes and took a breath, closing out the world around me. Suddenly, I saw myself back in the cold water of the quarry. I heard the Lord speak, "I'm moving you through an acclimation process."

With one line he spoke directly to my heart. So many times I had pleaded with him for something to change in my circumstance. For years it felt like things were heading in the opposite direction I had imagined them going. It seemed like once a month, a partner in ministry walked away from what we had been building. I had no sense of vision anymore. Anything I put my hands to seemed to fall apart. It felt as though the only solution was escape.

But he was inviting me deeper.

There is something that gets developed in us, in that struggle of acclimation. The work of going down and back up, again and again, is a necessary part of the process, it's what prepares us for a greater depth.

"Lord, I've faced this barrier for quite a while. I've been so frustrated by my inability to go deeper and further than where I've been. The pain of my circumstance feels like the barrier, it's preventing me from going anywhere." I kept telling myself, *Once I get out of here things will be better again.*

"It will be easier for you if you find an escape," I heard the Lord respond, "that's because you'll have settled for shallow waters. Feel free to do so!"

I sensed the sincerity of the offer and it unsettled me.

"But I am inviting you to deeper water. Your current struggle is the acclimation process. Embrace it! Learn to cultivate my presence and peace in the increased pressure and discomfort. You will not be able to be sustained in deeper water if you can't acclimate with me here."

When given the option, I know I'm not willing to settle for the shallow waters of where I've been. We were designed to go deeper. I am committed to the acclimation process.

How comfortable are we with *process*? The truth is, we tend to have a hard time with it. Why? We hold ourselves to certain standards of where we should be, what we should be capable of, and it seems that no matter where we are, we're never where we "should be." It's hard to live in process when we see where we want to be, but it seems so far away. There is a relief that comes in arriving, but if we can learn to engage in the journey, we're bound to discover beauty that we would have otherwise missed.

Complacency would be a much more comfortable way to live.

Have some initial success, then just live off of that success! It's very attractive, there's just no life in it. It seems as though God is more interested in our development than in our comfort. Complacency is like setting up camp in a current success when your general trained you for advancement.

Have you ever heard of Sears? Sears set up camp. The company came about when department stores were becoming a big hit. Sears boomed with success! However, it didn't last. They stopped innovating and they coasted off their previous success. Now, Sears is an endangered species in the jungle of consumerism.

It's a proven pattern for humanity that once we've tasted a level of success, we tend to settle into that level. We do this because it's comfortable, but also because to move forward would require that we risk what we've gained thus far. When we've accumulated very little, we're not afraid to put it on the line. But when the numbers begin to grow we start to shift our focus from growing to preserving.

Complacency is like carbon monoxide filling the house. We don't notice it until it kills us.

"You are old and advanced in years,
and there remains yet very much land to possess."
JOSHUA 13:1

So God gently knocks, and invites us back into the continual upward advancement our hearts were made for. Look at Psalm 1:32.

"The complacency of fools destroys them;
But whoever listens to me will dwell secure and will be at ease,
without dread of disaster."

Safety isn't found in preservation; it's found in following the *voice*. Success and security can cause us to disengage from God's voice and presence. The irony is that success and security result when we listen to the voice.

His leadership is the one nonnegotiable for our advancement. It's worth the loss of all progress gained.

John Wimber had learned the art of holding previous success loosely. At one point he left a successful music career. For a time, he found himself working as an assistant to a welder. Covered in grease, he was half in an oil drum when his music partner pulled up in a convertible with papers for John to sign. There, in the shop and in obscurity he signed away his royalties from the music they had created. Upon reflecting on this moment of his journey, Wimber explained,

> *The economy of the kingdom of God is quite simple. Every new step in the kingdom costs us everything we have gained to date. Every time we cross a new threshold, it costs us everything we now have. Every new step may cost us all the reputation and security we have accumulated up to that point. It costs us our life. A disciple is always ready to take the next step. If there is anything that characterizes Christian maturity, it is the willingness to become a beginner again for Jesus Christ. It is the willingness to put our hand in his hand and say, "I'm scared to death, but I'll go with you. You're the Pearl of great price."*

There is no greater advancement in the Kingdom than the Kingdom's advancement in you. When you seek first the Kingdom of God and his righteousness, you are drawn into the swirl of God's activity and the expressed power of his nature. What better circumstances are there beyond a continual flood of peace? What could you possibly possess that would surpass his bursting joy? What promotion could make you more secure, more fulfilled, than the experience of his lavishing love?

Advancement in the Kingdom of God is always available—in every waking moment—because God is always seeking to advance upon you. His goodness and mercy are always in pursuit of you. Surrender is the way forward. We advance when we lay down the results of yesterday's fight in absolute abandon.

For Melissa, advancement and surrender had always looked quite different than mine. I jumped into ministry on day one, but she stayed as far to the back of the room as possible. She always hated the stereotype of the *pastor's wife,* she would not be playing the piano or leading the children's ministry. There's not a bone in her body that would bend to the expectation of others.

She would, however, bend in worship. I was always astounded by the experiences she had with Jesus. Once when we were watching TV, a cheesy cologne commercial came on. A man and a woman were dancing in the moonlight, then suddenly they began to float. Soon they were soaring higher and higher, until they found themselves dancing on the moon.

I turned to her to mock the commercial when I noticed tears welling. "You okay babe?"

"I've done that with Jesus several times." Her face reddened as she noted my mouth open wide. "What?! I have. We danced in the moonlight without gravity. He's taken me flying several times. Sometimes He takes me on a tour through space." She grabbed a handful of my shirt to wipe her eyes. "It's beautiful."

I shook my head in disbelief. "I can't compete with that."

She laughed as she patted my wet shirt onto my stomach. "Oh there's no competition babe. Jesus is way more romantic than you."

I used to be so offended at her resistance to leading. However, during that time, Melissa developed a hidden depth with God that I eventually learned to appreciate. But the Lord was beginning to call her out into uncomfortable spaces. When we started SoKM, Melissa was determined to be on the leaders' team, because the leaders had a weeklong intensive training at the beginning of the year. She knew the intensive was going to be an opportunity to go deeper with the Lord, and somehow she managed a role on the team that kept her out of the spotlight.

Halfway through the first year, our Activator stepped down from the team. The Activator's job was to lead the class through exercises of listening to the Spirit in ministering to others. The Activator explained the exercise, then they modeled it in front of the class. When the Activator stepped down, we looked to Melissa to fill the role. She knew she was trapped. Even worse, she could sense Jesus inviting her forward. Melissa could resist anyone, but she could not resist Jesus.

Out of pure obedience, Melissa stepped forward and began leading from the front at SoKM. She was still resistant to leading on Sunday mornings, only occasionally I would convince her to share something or facilitate an exercise outside of SoKM. But the ball had begun to roll. Jesus was speaking identity over Melissa and inviting her to see how He wanted to partner with her for others.

The process accelerated for Melissa three years ago, when Putty invited us to go on an international ministry trip with his team. When we received the invitation, I was so excited at the possibility. But somehow I knew that the trip was for Melissa, not me. Our kids were young and two weeks was too long for them to be without both of us.

I said, "I think this trip is for you, babe. You should do it."

"No way! I'm not going without you," she was shaking her

head as she spoke. "If only one of us is going it's you."

I didn't fight her; I was too tired to fight. I headed for bed. Melissa sat up in bed, reading Putty's email again. Suddenly she remembered a dream she had just one week prior. In the dream, she was at some big church event with a team. She watched Putty walking onto the stage. He stopped and turned to Melissa, waving at her to follow him. She got up, following him up the steps onto the stage. He said to her, "Stay close, you're going to be ministering with me for a while."

As the dream continued, Melissa saw herself on stage in front of hundreds of people, sharing a prophetic word to someone she could see in the audience. She had an uncharacteristic calm as she shared what the Lord had told her.

She sat in the bed in shock. Remembering the dream was an instant confirmation that she knew was from the Lord. She would be going on the trip.

The clarity came with grief. This trip would mark another shift in her journey with the Lord that came with a loss. She never liked attention, and she had successfully avoided it for a long time. This was about to change.

On numerous occasions people had told her that they had seen a podium and a microphone. They would say things like, "God's given you a voice," and "God's giving you a platform, you're going to minister on a larger scale." She would smile politely, with an internal repulsion and terror.

Her whispered prayers drifted from the bed. "Father, I don't want to be seen. Can't I just stay hidden with you?" She closed her eyes, tuning into the Lord's presence.

She was swept into a vision. She was walking next to a lion, down a crowded street. Her attention was on the lion. He was majestic, beautiful, and radiating with power. With each step, a wave of muscle moved through Him. Her hand moved across His side. She gave no thought to whether she had permission, she was compelled to touch Him. He was firm, but his fur was soft and warm. She could reach her hand deep in His mane, His hair was rough.

Her attention shifted to the crowd along the side of the road. No one was afraid of the lion, only reverent. Suddenly she became aware that they were watching her with reverence as well. She began to feel anxious, realizing that they were as aware of her as they were the lion. *Why would they notice me next to Him?* She could feel panic starting to rise.

Then she noticed that her hand was still buried in His mane. It was so thick; she couldn't see past her forearm. She was gripping a clump of His hair. Immediately, calm settled over her. Somehow she felt safer, knowing that the crowd couldn't see her arm, hidden in the mane. The lion turned to her and said, "They won't ever see all of you. There will always be a part of you that's hidden if you don't let go."

With that the vision ended. She prayed a simple prayer, "Thanks," and drifted off to sleep. The next morning, she told me about her experience. I did a little celebration dance. She committed to the ministry trip. When the trip rolled around, I was surprised at how relaxed she was. She ended up leading a training on the trip, and came back excited to tell me how much she enjoyed it. This was not the Melissa I had known. Something had shifted in her.

I sat in my cove of The Depot, reflecting on Melissa's journey. My phone buzzed with a text from Andy, "I think we're due for another hike."

Andy and I knew each other in college, then worked together for a few years after, but we had never really been close. I didn't see him as someone who took life seriously, he always seemed so shallow. But recently he had taken a serious interest in hiking. The wilderness became a point of meaningful connection for both of us. We were both navigating painful situations and the temptation to run away.

I peeked my head around the corner and surveyed The Depot. Another pastor was meeting with someone whose back was toward me. He saw me, smiled, and waved. I waved back. I noticed a portrait of mountains on the wall above him. The setting sun cast an orange light on the landscape. Below the scene were the famous words of John Muir, "The mountains are calling, and I must go."

The words resounded in my heart. It was time to plan another wilderness adventure. I turned to my laptop and sent an email to my hiking companions.

CHAPTER 11

THE URGENCY OF NEARNESS

AFTER ANOTHER TRIP TO THE BATHROOM, I made my way slowly back to the bedroom. Everything hurt. My head pounded. It seemed that every muscle in my body was not happy. There wasn't much relief when I was submerged beneath the covers. Once a refuge, my bed had become a prison. It was day three of Covid. I was the first of the family to get it, but there were signs that Melissa was close behind.

In and out of consciousness, I would occasionally grab my phone off the nightstand and check my regular apps. One in particular had become a recent addiction: the stock market.

After the sale of our house earlier in the year, I had become a student of the stock market. Buying in at the start of the pandemic, I had quickly experienced a high yield that flooded my brain with endorphins. I was hooked.

Apparently however, the frequency at which you check your investments doesn't have any impact on their growth. It does however grow something else: anxiety. Over the past six months, my growing fascination with investment paid high dividends in anxiety. My ability to be present to those around me had diminished dramatically. I knew the constant checking wasn't helping my sense of peace, but I had allowed the ease of the process to enslave me.

Minutes passed, and I grabbed my phone again. Out of the silence I heard the subtle voice of the Lord, "Is this what you want to give yourself to?"

My heart was filled with grief at the question. Countless times over the years I had told the Lord how much I valued His voice. Countless times I had leaned in and sought Him out. I had fought against the things that compromised my ability to hear Him. But it had been a painful season, and I was tired of being present to the pain. The stock market, among other things, had offered an escape.

The grief turned to repentance, as I remembered myself. "Papa, I'm so sorry. I haven't honored your voice. Nothing matters more to me than to hear you, to know you and to stay close to you. You alone are my life. Please help me to value your voice above everything else."

Peace came over me as I took a breath and slipped back into sleep. An hour later I instinctively reached for my phone. I stopped myself, laughing. Melissa popped her head in the bedroom and smiled, "Hi little weakling, how ya doin?"

I smirked at her. "This is lame."

"Yea—" The kids screamed from downstairs. "I should probably check on that. You should check your email," she said.

Curious, I grabbed my phone as she headed downstairs. There was an email to both of us, from a leader of a church in Missouri that had mentored us over the past few years. I opened it up.

We're looking to bring a new couple on staff, with the hope of preparing them to take over the church in a few years. We think you two might be a great fit. Would you be willing to consider joining us in Aurora?

My mind shot in several directions. *This church is at least ten times the size of our current church. More importantly, there's a healthy culture and leadership team in place. This church shares so many of our values and convictions. This would be such a promotion! It would be quite a move; how would the kids handle it? Wait, what about our church, this has been such a fragile season, would they be ok?*

I said to myself, "I can't afford to consider this decision without hearing from you, Lord."

So many things in our lives compete for the seat of urgency. *You need to make this decision right now. You can't live one more day without this product. If you don't address this threat today, your world will implode.* We live in a world where politicians and products are constantly vying for our attention. Our emotions and circumstances often add to the noise. If we give in, we'll worship the one seated upon urgency with an offering of our attention.

Personally I've found that if I allow whatever situation to hold the seat of urgency, it rarely results well for anyone. If, however, I succeed in bringing my attention back to the Lord, I am much better equipped to walk in wisdom. I call this *the Urgency of Nearness.*

There's an urgency that trumps all others, and that's the crisis of our attention. The Lord is already near, but when I train my attention upon Him, I experience His nearness in all situations.

The Lord is at hand;
Do not be anxious about anything, but in everything,
By prayer and supplication with thanksgiving
Let your requests be made known to God.
And the peace of God, which surpasses all understanding,
Will guard your hearts and minds in Christ Jesus.
PHILIPPIANS 4:5-7

The Urgency of Nearness is where we resolve to give our attention solely to the only One who satisfies, preserves, protects, and promotes. Like Daniel's friends, we *pay no attention* to the threats that demand our worship (Daniel 3:12) and we lean into God's faithful nearness.

I took a breath, and I was reminded of what I had prayed an hour earlier, *help me to value your voice above everything else.* Suddenly the email felt like an answer to prayer. God was immediately giving me an opportunity to grow my value for his voice. The thought came to my mind. *This is training in the Urgency of Nearness.* I sat up in bed and made a vow to the Lord.

"God I refuse to make this decision apart from you. I'm not going to make this decision based on anything but your voice."

I thought of my little church family. I pictured telling Barbara that I was leaving, seeing her heart break. Barbara was in her late seventies, living alone. We had essentially adopted her into our family, inviting her over for meals. She would bring her stuffed animals and play with the kids. "Lord, I'm not willing to consider this job unless you tell me my church will be okay."

Without missing a beat, the Lord spoke to my heart, "What business is that of yours?"

"What do you mean?"

"It's not your church, it's mine. What happens to them isn't your business. Your business is to trust me and to follow me."

"So you're sending us to this other church?"

"I want you to begin the discernment process."

I headed downstairs and processed the email with Melissa. We decided to begin the conversation. We reached out to Deb, telling her about the opportunity and asked her to pray. After the mission trip to Guatemala, Deb began to take the role of a spiritual mom for us. We sought her out when we were facing a big decision or challenge. She listened patiently as we shared the details of the opportunity and said she would pray.

We began informal conversations with the leadership of the church in Aurora, then moved into formal interviews. We made several pros and cons lists, and sought counsel from wise leaders. Throughout the process we experienced such resonance between us and the team.

Everything seemed to be falling into place. The senior pastor was the type of leader I could work with. Others on the team shared our passion and were excited about the increasing likelihood that we would join. The handful of wise mentors we talked to were excited about what seemed like a clear next step for us.

Then we received a call from Deb. We put her on speakerphone.

"I've been praying for you guys about this." She paused.

"Yeah, are you hearing anything?"

Another pause. "Yeah," her tone was upbeat, but it seemed somewhat forced. "I feel like the Lord said that you're going, but it's not going to be what you think."

Melissa and I exchanged glances. *What does that even mean?*

I didn't like the sound of it. Our current assignment had been clearly from the Lord, but the last several years certainly hadn't played out how I thought it would. There had been so much disappointment. For a while it seemed there was a momentum, not just in our church but in our community. Then things shifted. *What had happened?* Every time I asked that question, grief and guilt would sweep over me again.

Deb's cautious affirmation did not sit well with me. What if God was kind enough to give us permission to rush to some shiny future, rather than face the unresolved pain of the present? That would bring some relief, but would we be signing up for a similar story in a different setting? We needed more clarity than that. We resolved to hold the prospect loosely. *Maybe we'll get the clarity we need when we visit the church in January.* We began to wonder out loud at the possibility of another option we hadn't seen yet, we called it, "Unknown option C."

On December fourth, I sat in the office of our house, writing an email to our leadership team. We had filled them in on the likelihood of an upcoming departure, now I wanted to encourage them. The decision was constantly on my mind, I wanted to know what we were doing, so I could begin the necessary work. My daughter knocked on the door behind me.

"Dad can we go sledding?"

I let out a loud sigh. "I can't right now, I'm working."

Melissa opened the door. "Dad," her eyes were wide, imploring me to remember my role in the family. "I think we all could use some time sledding." Her tone told me that this was more than a recommendation.

We had decided to homeschool the kids for a year when the pandemic hit. Working from home was torture. I sighed as I looked back at the computer. "Okay. I'll go get the sleds from the garage."

"Grab all of them please," she called after me in her sweet song voice. "I want options!" Melissa continued to help the kids put on their gear.

As I loaded the sleds, I grumbled, "Why do we have seven sleds anyway? There are only four of us!"

"Get over it, Dad!" my daughter yelled from the back seat.

It was the first snow of the season. Already the temperature was rising, the wet snow made the hill slick as we raced down.

Halfway down, the contour of the hill shifted, causing us all to turn in various directions. Between the contour and the snow-turned-to-ice, it was chaos. After the first few rides down the hill, Melissa and I collided at the bottom.

"Isn't this fun?!" she asked. "We have no way of knowing where we'll end up!"

"Yes!" Then it hit me. "What an accurate picture of our life right now." Things felt so out of control. No matter how hard we tried, we hadn't a clue where we were headed. I had become so obsessed about knowing what was next, that I was not living in the moment.

As I shredded the hillside, (nearly missing trees and family members), I found myself so thankful for the imagery the Lord had provided. It felt a bit as though the Lord was inviting me to hold tight to my sled—which I took to be a metaphor for Himself—and enjoy the ride. *"Hold tight and enjoy the ride."*

The four of us had the hill entirely to ourselves until a Volkswagen pulled up at the base of the hill. Two kids came scrambling up the hill. The four of us watched as they made their way, slipping as they came. As they came closer I saw that instead of sleds, one had a diaper changing pad, the other had a bus tub from a restaurant. Melissa and I looked at each other, then down to the extra sleds at our feet. *Oh. That's why we brought those.*

We greeted the two boys, watched them attempt the hill with their creative sled alternatives, then offered them some of ours. They delightfully accepted. Within minutes these two kids—who we'd never met, were engrafted into our family on the hillside. They would wait with our kids as Melissa and I trudged back up to the top for the next round. How invigorating! It felt like our family was getting to be who God made us to be together.

The oldest kid waited for me at the top. "Wanna race?"

"Yeah!"

"It's my birthday next week." Before I could respond he darted down the hill on my childhood sled.

I raced to catch up, sliding next to him at the bottom. "What's your name?"

"Myron. That's my brother Josh."

"Myron, I don't think I've ever met a Myron. How old are you gonna be next week?"

"Eight!"

"How cool! Hey Myron, that sled you have is my birthday present to you. It's called the Ziffy Whomper. Happy birthday!"

He yelled over his shoulder, "Okay!" as he ran back up the hill.

I had had that sled for over twenty-five years. I remember being on the front page of the paper on that sled. I can't describe the joy I experienced in giving my Ziffy Whomper to Myron. He was oblivious to it, which somehow made it better. We said farewell to our new friends and we headed home for hot chocolate.

Our snow gear was scattered through the house as we sipped hot chocolate. My phone rang. It was Job and Family Services. We had recently finished our foster care certification, and had been waiting for our first placement. I answered. The director explained that they had an emergency placement for a three-month-old boy. She gave me the details, and I asked, "What's his name?"

"His name is Myron."

My eyes went wide. "I'll have to call you back." I had never met anyone with that name before two hours ago. What are the chances this kid has the same name as the one who now has my beloved Ziffy Whomper? I heard the whisper of the Spirit, *Hold tight and enjoy the ride.* I called Melissa into the office and told her about the emergency placement.

"We can't take a baby right now! We need to figure out what we're doing with our lives!"

I reminded her of what I had heard the Lord say at the hill. *Hold tight and enjoy the ride.* "You'll never guess the baby's name."

"What is it?"

"Myron."

She went still. "Are we seriously gonna take a baby right now?"

"It seems like the Lord, doesn't it? Babe, it's so clear to me, I feel like it would be wrong to say no."

She sighed. "At least explain to the director that we could be moving in six months. She might not want to place the baby with us if she knows that."

I called the director back. Apparently she didn't care. "Great! We'll bring him to you within the hour."

With the arrival of little Myron, our lives came to a sudden halt. Nothing else mattered as we dove back into the world of midnight feedings and dirty diapers. His innocent laugh was enough to derail any train of thought. We had three months with Myron. Our time with him altered the course of our family.

I wanted the Lord to give me clarity on a big life decision. Instead he gave me a baby. I wanted the Lord to meet me with answers to my questions, instead He gave me more chaos. My grip began to loosen on the demand for answers. The urgency of making a life decision dissipated under the weight of moment by moment demands. Myron positioned me for a dramatic shift in my heart.

Myron was the beginning of a downward spiral of surrender.

Around the time Myron was reunited with his mom, the day came to visit the prospective church in Aurora. The visit was anticlimactic. The church was better than we imagined, and we felt connected to the team. Yet we shared a sense that the Lord was telling us to wait. We told the pastor what we sensed, and he shared our confusion. We drove home disappointed at the lack of closure or clarity.

CHAPTER 12

THE FLOW OF GRACE

WITH OUR SHOES IN HAND and packs on our backs, we crossed the wide stream at the base of Breathed Mountain. The frigid water moved quickly, making it nearly impossible to grip the slick rocks with our bare feet. The crossing was a buffet of sensations. The rocks beneath the surface varied with every step, some smooth, some sharp, some firm, some loose. Every step was a slow surprise as we found our footing. The shock of the cold shot up from our feet, causing our whole bodies to tense while the warmth of the setting sun greeted any exposed skin above the surface. Spurts of laughter broke out in every direction, as we watched each other stumble, fighting to keep our packs dry.

We sat on the other side, swinging our feet in the sun to dry before slipping on our shoes. I looked at the guys around me. It was often such an eclectic mix when we went backpacking. Some were pastors, some worked in insurance, children's services, or construction. Typically, we all had two things in common. One, we loved adventure. And two, we wanted to grow in our ability to hear from God. These short trips into the wilderness offered a respite from the mundane, where God had space to break in.

God tends to break in when we gather with others in ways He can't when we're alone. There's a fascinating dynamic when we gather with others who are leaning into the Lord in their own journeys. The Spirit is moving uniquely upon and within each of us, and when we come closer together, those unique movements begin to mingle and meld. This dynamic creates a new layer of grace; of the Spirit speaking and moving among us. There are rich nutrients available in the space among us.

Over the next few miles, pockets of conversation developed and dispersed along the trail. Jeff and I resumed our conversation as we continued down the trail.

A skillet swung on the right side of his pack, occasionally clinking against his metallic water bottle. We love to tease him, his pack is always the heaviest, but when it comes time for dinner the teasing stops. He's a masterful chef on the trail. *Chef Jeff.* I've been hiking with Jeff for over ten years now. He's one of the safest people I know. Behind his round glasses, his soft eyes and his warm smile invite vulnerability.

"So, have you decided what you're gonna do?"

I let out a sigh. "Honestly, it's confusing. I could name so many reasons why we should take the job in Aurora. But something isn't sitting right."

"What do you mean?"

I looked ahead. Rays of sun popped through the cracks in the canopy of trees. "When I think about that church, it's literally an answer to so many things I've asked for. And I have a clear sense that God would totally bless it if we went there. But deep down, I feel a more subtle invitation…to trust the Lord and remain in the unknown."

"Why would He do that?"

I shook my head. "I don't know. I don't want to do that! I'm so tired of the unknown!" It hurt to admit, but Jeff didn't correct me. He gave a grunt of understanding.

We walked in silence. The trail was so saturated; each step was accompanied by a squish. Occasionally the skillet clinked against the water bottle over the distant sounds of conversation ahead and behind. A third set of squishes came into rhythm with ours; Luke. Luke was a full six inches taller than Jeff and I, which he used to his full advantage when we played basketball. We were okay with it though, his hugs are the best, even if we were getting a face full of armpit.

The three of us had a rich history together. We had spent several years serving in various leadership capacities in a Presbyterian church. Luke was the senior pastor (who introduced me to beer), I was the youth pastor, and Jeff was a campus minister at a local college. We'd get together once a week to play racquetball. It was an excellent way of dealing with stress. Some days we'd hit the ball as hard as we could, letting our rage fly. The court became a weekly refuge, where we could be real and raw with our frustrations. Now we've gone our separate ways, and backpacking is our annual reunion.

Jeff looked to Luke. "How's your church going Luke?"

Luke responded with a low growl.

I laughed. "That good huh?"

He forced a chuckle. "I feel like I have been reduced to a professional fryer operator. People come to church, expecting certain products, and I make the fries. I'm so tired of McChurch."

Jeff's eyes went wide. "I don't like that."

"That's consumerism for you," I chimed in. "Sucks when the Church falls into it."

Luke continued. "Yeah, and Covid has made it even more obvious."

"How so?" I asked.

"In the midst of a global pandemic, people in the church just try to find a way to keep providing the same products. So we broadcast our sermons. Instead of passive participants sitting in pews, people watch from the comfort of the couch in their pajamas."

Jeff added, "McChurch makes discipleship nearly impossible."

"It's not a product. It's not a performance," Luke paused, shaking his head. "Why do we make it so pastor-central?"

The question poked at me. "Two verses have been haunting me since the beginning of the pandemic. 1 Corinthians 12:7, 'To *each* has been given a manifestation of the Spirit for the common good.' and Ephesians 4:7, 'But grace was given to *each one* of us according to the measure of Christ's gift.' I feel like so much of the church in the west limits the flow of the Spirit to a selection of professional people in the room, like a narrow funnel. How do we widen the funnel?"

I waited for them to throw stones at me. They walked in silence. "The Church is the gathering of the saints, right?"

Jeff nodded. "Jesus said that when two or three gather, He's there with them."

"When saints gather, God makes it His temple. He comes among us, and there's a flow of His grace between us. So the flow of grace was never meant to be limited to the expert."

Suddenly I became aware that the conversation of the group behind us had died down, more pairs of squishes were joining our stride. I looked back at Mark. He smiled at me.

"What if our job as leaders is less about having a lot to say, and more about increasing the flow of grace among us?" I said.

"Decentralization." Luke chimed in. He stopped suddenly and began flailing his arms as if fighting an invisible enemy. We all laughed as he cleared the trail of spider webs. He continued, "There needs to be a shift from the expert and the performer, to a room full of grace carriers."

"It makes me think of Airbnb or Uber." Jeff chimed in. "Centralized experts used to have a monopoly on these services, now anybody can provide a room or a ride! But what would this look like for the church?"

"I have no idea," I confessed. "But I think it starts with a willingness to sacrifice things that have been central for so long. Can we let go of the building, of a Sunday morning time slot, a sermon, a weekly offering?"

"You guys are describing my church." All heads turned. Mark walked in the back of the group.

"What do you mean?" Jeff asked.

"Decentralization." Mark paused, looking at us with a smile. He was clearly enjoying the suspense. "Some Sundays we don't even meet as a church. The large gathering—as we call it, isn't the main thing we do."

"Well then what is?" I asked.

"We call them MCs, or *missional communities*,"[1] Andy explained. He was walking next to Mark. They had come together, but I didn't know they were a part of the same church. "They're like house churches or small groups. We meet in homes. Sometimes it's a Bible study, sometimes it's prayer and worship. Sometimes we go out into the community and serve."

"Sometimes we just hang out," Mark added. "We might have a cookout, or a day at the beach. The MCs are the lifeblood of our church. We actually encourage participation in an MC more than

---

1 Mark and Andy's church was highly influenced by Mike Breen, *Leading Missional Communities*

the large gathering on Sunday morning."

The pastors in the group were silent.

Jeff spoke up, "I like it."

Luke and I murmured our agreement.

"It's getting dark. We should probably stop soon," someone said.

"There's a campsite on the other side of this creek," I explained.

Little was said as we all busied ourselves around the campsite. Some set up hammocks or tents, while others searched for dry firewood. The site was between two streams that angled and converged just south of camp. There was something peaceful about the noise of streams that surrounded us. Luke and Mark worked on getting a fire roaring as Chef Jeff began to set up for dinner.

After stuffing our bellies with spicy chicken and rice, we sat around the fire, on rocks or logs, some with our backs against trees. A few of us got out our flasks of whiskey, passing them around for samples. These are sacred moments, where trust has been earned, and friends can be enjoyed without the distraction of screens or the tyranny of the urgent. I am certain that moments like these are a window. We are glimpsing something of the nature of heaven.

As the guys began to move away from the fire, preparing for bed, I was drawn to the creek. I found a large, flat boulder in the middle and made my way to it. I looked up and I was met by a wide backdrop of bright stars. I stood, gazing at their beauty until my neck hurt.

"Mind if I join you?" Andy was standing at the edge of the creek, silhouetted by the fire. In the firelight I could faintly make out his hat. It had white mesh in the back, and camo in the front with Cleveland Browns front and center. I didn't understand that combination. It reminded me that I didn't have Andy figured out, he didn't fit any stereotypes.

"Of course." I pointed to the path of rocks I had taken to cross.

He hopped across and stood next to me. He took a big breath as he looked up. "Man, it's beautiful out here. Thank you for inviting me."

"Funny, I don't remember inviting you!" We laughed.

Andy and I had gone to college together, but it had been over a decade. We barely knew each other then, even less since. But he had seen various pictures I had shared on social media, and finally reached out and asked if he could come on a trip. I'm so glad he did.

"Has God told you whether you're supposed to go to that church yet?"

"No, and it's really irritating me. I'm starting to think He's not going to tell me either way."

"Heh. Yeah, that sounds about right."

"Huh? Why?"

"Do you think He wants you to just do what He tells you?"

I looked up at the stars. "That's the way I want it to work, but no. I don't think that's what He wants. Isn't there a verse, something about a bit and bridle?"

"Yeah, we were just looking at this a few weeks ago in our MC. It's in the psalms, hold on!" He crossed to camp and grabbed something from his pack. A minute later he came back, flipping the pages of his journal in the light of his headlamp.

"These verses so struck me, I wrote them down. 'I will instruct you and teach you in the way you should go; I will counsel you with my eye upon you. Be not like a horse or mule, without understanding, which must be curbed with bit and bridle, or it will not stay near you.'"

I pondered those words as we looked back up at the stars.

Andy took a breath. "It seems like God doesn't tell us what to do at every turn, because He wants to cultivate us in wisdom more than He wants to see us make all the *right* decisions."

"Say what?"

"Kyle, what if this big, hard decision is less about which way is right, and more about what He's cultivating in you?"

"I don't know how I feel about that."

"He's a Father right? Well, He wants mature sons. Sons can't mature unless they're given freedom and power to make decisions. He wants sons who, because they know His heart, have an innate capacity and desire to make decisions that reflect Him even when He's not directing."

I shook my head as I took a deep breath. "It's terrifying how much trust God gives us, man. I feel like there are so many moments in my life that would have worked out better if He would have just told me what to do."

"But I wonder what was cultivated in you in those moments. Or in the moments that followed, as you've looked back on mistakes and failures. If you've learned from them, those were probably some of the most formative moments of your life."

I put my hands on the temples of my head as I looked again at the sky. "When I think about this current season, I can see how He's cultivating deep things in me."

"Like what?"

"Definitely deeper trust. I couldn't grow in trust without some unknowns."

Andy turned to me and smiled.

We stood there and allowed the sound of the stream and the starry sky to take the center stage. Eventually the cold night drove us to our sleeping bags. I laid there, revisiting the conversations of the day. My framework for this decision was shifting quickly, and with it came new questions. The central question at the moment was clear: *What is God cultivating in me?*

I faded to sleep in my swinging hammock, with a looser grip on the desire for clarity.

CHAPTER 13

LOOKING FOR THE GRACE

I WOKE TO THE SOUND of movement in the camp. One drawback of sleeping in a hammock in the wilderness is how vulnerable it feels. Whenever I hear sounds of movement near me, I picture a bear, drooling, with a fork in his hand. He's looking at me in my hammock like a fresh sausage link swinging in the breeze. I peeked out from behind the material.

Chef Jeff was working on restarting the fire. He looked far less threatening than a bear. I laid back in the hammock. It was too chilly; I'd wait till the fire was started. On second thought, my bladder had other opinions. Over the next hour, each of us emerged one by one going about our own morning routines.

Some mornings are slower and more relaxed. Guys will often bring along a book or a journal, and strike off to a solitary spot for contemplation. But when it's cold, we're typically a little more motivated to get moving. It's a snowball effect on a cold morning like this. Everyone watches one another's progress, if one person starts to pack up camp, others follow. No one wants to be the last one while all the others sit around waiting. Except for Dustin. He marches to the beat of his own drum. Or in this case, he sleeps to the sound of his own snore.

A few of us enjoyed coffee and oatmeal by the fire. Adam stopped packing and walked up to us. He whispered, "Guys, watch this."

Andy fell in line and the two of them tip-toed toward Dustin's hammock. Dustin's snoring stopped abruptly, as if he could sense danger. Andy and Adam stopped in their tracks, now everyone was watching. Adam held up three fingers to Andy to signal a countdown.

"Arrrrrr!" The two of them growled.

Dustin's hammock shook and swirled as he yelled. He fell halfway out and looked at us. His eyes were wide and his hair was wild as he hung upside down, taking in the scene. Adam and Andy were doubled over, laughing.

"You guys are punks," Dustin grumbled as he climbed back into his hammock.

Thirty minutes later, we were all packed up and ready to continue the trail. With our packs strapped, we stood around the fire ring. Dustin prayed a blessing over the campsite. I can't remember who started this ritual, but it's become a part of our trips. Campsites become sacred spaces, and we want others to experience God's presence there.

Jeff pulled out his map. "We're uh… here we are. We'll be on this trail for about another four miles, then we'll turn onto this trail, which will eventually run parallel with Canaan Valley. We should have a pretty good view from the top by lunch."

"Can I give you guys a question to ponder for the day?" Luke asked as we started down the trail. He continued as we all mumbled our consent. "C.S. Lewis says that 'Myth has the ability to communicate truth in a way that facts do not.' So, here's my question: what "mythic" character is a reflection of who God made you to be, and why?"

Luke's question has become a personal favorite of mine. When we're walking with God, He redefines us. The New Testament defines us as "In Christ," and therefore a new creation. We can continue to see ourselves as broken sinners, but we'd just be disagreeing with God. That's why the Holy Spirit's job is to convict us of righteousness (John 16:10).

He's not showing us what's wrong with us so much as what's right with us. He invites us to live more fully from who we really are now, with Jesus. Mythic characters have a way of showing us clues of the glory of God hidden within us.

"What do you mean by *mythic character?*" Adam asked.

"Think of a character from a story—a book, show or movie," Luke explained. "You don't have to answer it now. Think about it. Ask God how He sees you, and see if He brings a particular character to—"

"Jim Halpert!" Adam yelled from the front of the group.

"Wow, that was fast," Luke replied. "What about him?"

"He came to my mind right as you asked the question. My first thought was, *Who are you to compare yourself to him?* But I knew that was just shame talking… Uh, give me a moment." He paused. We walked in silence as Adam considered the question. "Jim is loyal to those around him. He's quick to prank Dwight, but ultimately he cares about him. He has dreams, but he's willing to sacrifice his own goals and ambitions for the greater good of his community."

Dustin hollered from the back, "I'd be willing to be your Dwight, Adam. Bears, beets, *Battlestar Galactica*."

Everyone laughed.

The group was silent as we began to find a rhythm for the morning. Gradually, the group spread out according to preferred paces and new pockets of conversation emerged. Mitch and I walked together in the middle of the pack.

Mitch surveyed the area we were walking through. We had quickly moved from a pine forest to an open clearing, with piles of boulders every few hundred yards. "So Kyle, I have a question for you."

I couldn't help but smile at his declarative tone.

Mitch noticed my smirk. "What?"

"You do that a lot. You say it like an announcement, usually those same words, *So Kyle, I have a question for you.* When you do it, I just know you've been thinking about something, and you're about to let me in on your process."

He laughed. "Am I that predictable?"

"Not really." I smiled. "What's your big question?"

"I overheard you talking about grace yesterday. You said something about each of us having *grace*. What do you mean by that?"

I adjusted my pack, shifting more of the weight to my hips. "Well, typically when we talk about 'grace,' we're talking about salvation or forgiveness, right?"

"Right. What's that verse? 'It is by grace you have been saved.' It's supposed to be a gift from God."

"Yeah, that's a perfect example. Grace is simply a gift from God. It's an expression of His kindness and favor towards us. The most famous example is forgiveness and salvation in Jesus. But that's not the only gift we receive from God."

Suddenly there was a loud gasp behind us, followed by laughter. Dustin was picking himself up from the ground, his face a little red. The others were laughing, looking back and forth between Dustin and the other side of the trail. There must have been some kind of critter, a few of the guys had their phones out, taking pictures.

Mitch and I kept moving, creating more space from the group behind us. "So what other kind of grace is there?"

"Right," I said, trying to regain my thought. "Grace is also an empowering or equipping. Have you ever read *The Chronicles of Narnia?*"

"I saw the movie."

"Do you remember when the kids met Santa?"

"Yeah," Mitch grinned. "That was sort of weird."

"Right? Didn't expect to find Santa in Narnia. But he is a representation of the Holy Spirit in that scene. He comes on the scene, bursting with hope and joy, and he brings gifts!"

"Doesn't he give weapons to the kids?"

I nodded. "A sword and shield, bow and arrows, and a small jar of some sort of healing potion."

"I think there were more, but I can't remember."

"The point is, they were each given gifts, specific to them, to equip them. They would eventually need those for the battles to come."

"Give me a minute." Mitch stopped, took off his pack, and knelt to tie his shoe. "So what does that story have to do with grace?"

"Okay, you know how Paul talks about the body of Christ?"

"Sure," Mitch responded as he finished tying his shoe. "The eye needs the nose and the foot needs the spleen and all that."

"If the spleen is mentioned I'll give you ten dollars," I laughed. "Well, one of the times Paul talks about the body, he says, 'having gifts that differ according to the grace given to us, let us use them.' He goes on to describe a few of them, like prophecy, teaching, faith…"

"So you're saying, grace is also like the weapons the kids received in Narnia?" Mitch asked, as he clipped his pack around his waist.

"I think so. God gives each of us assignments, and He equips us for those assignments," I said as we continued walking again.

"So how does this connect to your big decision?"

"It's funny, I'm not quite sure. But I know it does. Recently Melissa and I were talking with another couple we know, who are sort of mentors to us. We were telling them how we weren't sure what was next for us, but that for some reason we just knew a change was coming. When we said that, the wife said, 'ah, so the grace is lifting huh?'"

Mitch burrowed his brow. "What's that supposed to mean?"

"I had no clue. So I asked. She explained, 'Well, sometimes you can tell that God is shifting your assignment, because you can feel the grace lifting off of you for your current assignment.'"

"And what does that mean to you?"

"Actually, it has helped me frame how I've been feeling over the past year. We love our church and our community! But the role I'm in, leading a church the way it currently is, doesn't quite fit anymore."

"Makes me think of David, when he tries on Saul's armor."

"I guess. The work I do used to fit me so well. But I've changed, and my understanding has changed. Now, the way the church currently functions feels heavy and ill-fitting."

Mitch's eyes widened, "It might fit perfectly for someone somewhere, but your assignment is different, and so your grace is different."

I let out a sigh. "*And*, that's why we can't take this position at the church in Aurora. It's a great offer, but it would be ill-fitting."

Suddenly I had the clarity I had been looking for. It wasn't what I expected, and honestly, it wasn't what I wanted.

I let that discovery sink in as we trudged along. We made our way up the gentle slope, through a wide open meadow on the side of the mountain. Here too, the ground was saturated, making some sections marsh-like with large puddles either to be circumnavigated or plowed through. The trail turned back into the woods, where we met up with Mark and Andy. They were stopped at an intersection, looking for something on the ground.

I asked, "Did you guys lose something?"

Andy responded like a kid getting his sibling in trouble, "Mark broke his pack."

"I did not!" Mark waved toward Andy, "Ignore him. One of my straps broke off the pack. We're looking for the metal clip to try to put it back together."

Mitch picked up the broken strap, investigating the break. "I have something that I think might fix it." He unzipped a pocket in his pack and pulled out his keys. He disconnected a key ring and used it to connect the strap back to its metal opening on the pack. "Voila."

Mark gave him a nod of approval. "Nice! Thanks."

I eyed Mark suspiciously. "Mark, aren't you an engineer? How long were you going to look for that clip?"

Andy burst out laughing.

"Alright, alright. I would have figured it out, I was just hoping to find the clip!"

Hours later, our hike culminated in the discovery of a campsite in a grid of pines near an overlook, well off trail. The rocky cliff-top gave us a view of the valley we had camped in the night before. With the sun setting on the other side of the valley, we stood in silence, taking in the scene around us. As night came in, we set up camp.

"Have you thought about my question?" Luke asked as we settled in around the fire. "I'm curious to hear what mythic character you relate to."

"Actually, yeah. I think I'm on to something." Mitch was the first to answer. "I've been thinking about it since Mark's pack broke—"

"You're MacGyver aren't you?" Andy broke in.

"Hehe, not quite, but similar. I'm Bruce Wayne." He surveyed our faces as he paused.

Adam looked confused. "Don't you mean Batman?"

"Sort of. Bruce Wayne has an abundance of wealth, and he's almost completely alone. He sees something wrong in his city and he decides to put his resources to good use. I have been learning a lot about finances over the years, and I want more and more to steward the resources that I've been entrusted with." He paused, looking at the fire. No one spoke. It seemed as though Mitch was deciding whether to share more. He looked up at us, then back down and continued. "Bruce also hides behind the mask. He lives two separate lives. He tries very hard to keep them separated. But eventually the two worlds collide, and he has to face the complexity, all the while figuring out who he truly is."

"Many people misjudge him," I said, watching Mitch as he avoided eye contact. "But those who really know him trust him with their lives." Mitch looked up, across the fire and smiled.

"I have one." Our attention turned to Jeff. "So, hear me out. Lucy from *Chronicles of Narnia*."

"Bold move, comparing yourself to a little girl while sitting around a fire with a bunch of guys." Mark said, as he poked at the fire. "Why Lucy?"

"Sometimes she sees things that no one else sees, and no one believes her. This creates problems, and grief for her. But as she grows in her confidence, she cares less about whether others believe her, because she's so drawn to follow Aslan when he reveals himself to her. I think God's given me an ability to see things that others can't see, and it allows me to follow God into places that only I can perceive."

Luke reached his hand out to Mark, who handed him the fire poking stick. He poked at the fire. "Well, mine might make you feel a little better about comparing yourself to a little girl, Jeff."

"Oh yeah? Let's hear it."

Luke dragged out his words, "I…am…an Ent."

"The trees from *The Lord of the Rings?*"

"Uh huh. The Ents are slow, deliberate, with lots of inertial energy. They are slow to get moving and slow to stop. This means frustration for their allies at first and ultimate victory over the second tower once they get moving. At their best, they are unstoppable. At their worst, they are unstartable. The Ents are entirely other, in some ways detached from the flow of the story. Yet in the end they are instrumental to victory."

"Reminds me of lava," Dustin replied, staring at the fire.

Luke handed the stick to Andy. Andy examined it, then began to rearrange logs on the fire. "I'm thinking Strider, from *Lord of the Rings*. He was a wandering, wounded soldier in the wilderness, who became a beloved hero." Andy looked at the faces around the fire. "The craziest thing though, was that he was a King the whole time. We watch him go through a journey of discovering who he is."

"Such a powerful picture of our identity in Christ," I said thoughtfully. "We're just on a journey of discovering who we are in Him."

Luke looked at me with curiosity. "Kyle, what about you?"

CHAPTER 14

ONE AND THE SAME

I DIDN'T ANSWER LUKE'S QUESTION. I made a joke and passed it off to someone else. I headed for the hammock early, I needed some time alone. My thoughts drifted to *The Lion King*.

Simba was always meant to be king. As a cub, he underwent training in character and strength that would prepare him for the throne. Until his father's tragic death. To make matters worse, his power hungry uncle convinced Simba that he could not be trusted. Scar caused Simba to question his own heart and to run for the hills. After a life of ease, Simba's love interest finds him. Seeing his odd behavior, she becomes a prophetic voice. *This is not who you are.*

Another prophet comes on the scene, Rafiki the monkey. He gets Simba's attention with a promise of seeing his father, and leads Simba to the greatest discovery of his life. The climax of the story takes place beside a stream. Simba encounters his father, who speaks identity over Simba. *You are my son, and the one true king.* Simba has not done anything of significance to speak of, yet his father speaks the most powerful affirmation over him. *I claim you as mine. You are just like me, and everything I have is yours.*

For Simba, this moment is the intersection of security and significance. The trauma and accusations of his childhood caused him to believe that he was rejected and untrustworthy. Now he was perceiving his value in the voice of his father. The declaration of his father is everything Simba needs to propel him from the wastelands back to his "people."

Like young Simba, the Father announces His pleasure over Jesus before He's really done anything of note. Also in a stream, during Jesus' baptism His Father declared,

> You are my beloved Son;
> With you am I well pleased.
> LUKE 3:22

We get it so backwards. We think we need to *do something* significant in order to *be somebody*. This is the mindset of an orphan. A son, however, knows who they are. They are secure, not because they've earned it, but because they've received it. Security is a superpower. When we know that we are loved and that we've been given value, we don't have to prove anything. We have nothing to lose. There isn't a question of whether we have anything to offer, because we have the DNA of our Father.

With the fire and conversation in the background, I laid in the hammock with my thoughts. I was reminded of a meeting with my church leadership a few years back.

I had been the pastor for three years, and the church wasn't growing. My full-time salary had been a stretch for their budget, and I felt so guilty for it. I told them I wanted to go part-time because I found handyman work to be therapeutic. It wasn't a lie, but I also felt so undeserving. I knew I wasn't doing a great job. While

I could preach, I didn't know how to lead. They asked me to leave the room while they discussed it. I headed outside for a walk.

As I walked, a song came to my mind. I knew it was from the Lord. As I walked I pulled out my phone and played "Born Again" by Cory Asbury. The lyrics pierced my heart, giving me my moment by the stream like Simba and Jesus.

And in the quiet pride of my Father's eyes,
I remember who I am
And when I feel the warmth of my Father's smile
Feels like I've been born again.

I could imagine the Father watching me with pride in His eyes; His face full of joy. I cried as I walked, feeling the warmth of my Father's delight and pride in me. That moment was an intersection for me, between security and significance. I didn't need to see any evidence of who I was, I knew it. I would take that depth of security with me everywhere I went, whether it was a stage in front of masses or the tightest corner of an attic. I was a beloved son. I looked like my Dad, and He was proud of me.

The memory washed over me as I lay in the hammock. I whispered a prayer, *I don't need to lead a big church. I just want to be your son. The greatest place of significance for me is wherever I can be more fully with you, Papa.* Warm from the Father's affection, I drifted to sleep, and I dreamed.

The dream was familiar; I had been in this place before. I was standing on a trail I had hiked alone two years ago. Oddly enough, it was a spot on the trail that I had not paid attention to when I was there in real life. I had hurried along this trail, on my way to see a swelling river in the middle of a gorge in North Carolina. The river was a powerful force to be reckoned with. It was massive, from the heavy rainfall, the effect of a hurricane coming up the coast. I had hoped to cross it but found it to be impossible. I was overwhelmed by the enormity and speed of the violent force of nature.

The river however was not the scene of the dream. Instead, I was about a mile away from the river, where a little tributary crossed the trail. Warm, heavy rain fell as I stood next to the small stream. I observed the little trickle, likely only recognizable during a heavy rainfall. I considered the dramatic contrast between this little flow and the massive river I knew was not far away. Then I noticed Jesus.

He was on the other side of the stream. He was also considering the stream. As I saw Him, looking at the stream with a sense of wonder, I realized that I had been looking at it with disdain. He seemed to see something I didn't see. He had the same awe as he looked at the stream, as I had when I had studied the river.

He looked up at me from the other side. He said, "They are one and the same." His whole face was smiling and His eyes were gentle. He continued, "I make no distinction between where it is and where it will be." I looked down at the stream then back at Him. His eyes stayed steadily on me.

I awoke, with the details of the dream vivid in my mind. I could hear the soft murmur of some of the others trying to reignite the fire. The crisp air stung my exposed face. I pulled the sleeping bag over me and worked to remember the progression of the dream.

Jesus was talking about He and I. I am that little trickle, but He sees me just as I see Him. If I didn't hear it from Jesus, I would have refused this point. It was clear that He believed what He said. I see the great contrast between who Jesus is and who I am, but Jesus doesn't see it that way. Jesus looks at me the same way I look at Him. It's as though Jesus truly believes that He is *now* my life.

For you have died,
And your life is hidden with Christ in God.
When Christ, who is your life appears,
Then you also will appear with Him in glory.
COLOSSIANS 3:3-4

Rivers are formed by tributaries. In the Kingdom of God, something miraculous takes place. The nature of the River transforms the tributaries. When we are joined to Christ, we become tributaries who are joined with the river ahead of our time. What we will be informs who we are now. Jesus has brought our new nature into the present, by placing us in Himself.

When we give ourselves to Christ, we lose our right to self-identify as a sinner. That is what we *were*. That version of us has died. Paul tells us that when we were baptized, we were buried with Jesus (Romans 6:3-4). He goes on to clarify further, saying our old self was crucified with Jesus. Then he goes on to give his first instruction in the entire book of Romans so far, "*consider* yourselves dead to sin and alive to God in Christ Jesus." (Romans 6:11)

Our being is no longer defined by our history. It's not defined by those ongoing mistakes and flaws you have that drive you nuts. It's defined only by the person of Jesus, *who is your life.*

How can this be true if I'm still a mess? We can live from who we were, or we can learn to live from who we are. In Colossians 3 Paul defines the readers as those who are seated with Christ in the heavenlies. They have died, and Christ is now their life. Then in verses 5-9 he describes the current mess of their lifestyle; distorted sexuality and desires, envy, malice, slander, etc. I find it interesting that the list ends with *lying.* If we're not paying attention, we simply see lying as part of the list.

"Do not lie to one another, seeing that you have put off the old self with its practices and have put on the new self, which is being renewed in knowledge, after the image of its creator."

Paul is not simply adding another bad practice to the list, he's describing what we're doing when we engage in these things.

When you do these things, you're lying to one another about who you are. The truth is that you have put off the old self and you have put on the new self.

How do we make this shift? How can we live from who we are rather than who we were?[1] It's not from striving. You can't will yourself to do good and not do bad. We need to learn to think differently. We are *transformed by the renewing of our minds* (Romans 12:1-2). This is the process of repentance; aligning our thoughts with God. When we seek to walk with God in our everyday lives, the Holy Spirit regularly brings to our attention faulty ways that we are thinking, and enables us to make a mental shift. We let go of old ways of seeing and receive new truths to build our lives upon.

I climbed out of my hammock and put on my winter cap. I gave a quick greeting as I walked past the fire ring. Before oatmeal and coffee, I wanted to visit the rocky cliff-top near camp. As I stepped out from the coverage of the pines, the crisp air of the open cliffs greeted me. I zipped up my jacket and put my hands in the pockets as I moved toward the edge. The wilderness seemed to have a life of

1 There is no way I could fully address these questions here! I have come across several excellent books on the topic of identity. Here are two that I highly recommend: *Live Like Jesus* by Putty Putman, and *Identity Matters* by Terry Wardle

its own. The rhythm of the wind through the trees created an eerie resemblance to the sound of breathing. *Breathed Mountain.*

I looked down. The steep drop-off gave a fantastic view of the open landscape. The river snaked through the valley, complete with rapids and pools. As I watched the river, I considered Jesus's words. *I make no distinction.*

I've always loved the imagery of Jesus as a river. One of my favorite descriptions of Jesus is in Isaiah,

> For he will come like a rushing stream,
> Which the wind of the Lord drives.
> Isaiah 59:19

If He and I are united now, what's true of Him is true of me. I will come like a rushing stream, which the wind of the Lord will drive. That rushing stream has the power to change the topography. It can literally *move mountains*. I have no idea where I'm headed with my life. But I do know one thing. The greatest place of impact I can ever have is where I can fully be who I am, with Christ.

To my left the rocky cliffs jutted out and formed what looked like the face of a lion. He looked tranquil, overlooking his territory as though there wasn't a threat in his world. He was royalty. I imagined I was Simba, standing next to my dad, admiring his majesty.

I raised my hands. The cold wind moved through my fingers. The sensation shot through my body like electricity, awakening every part of me. *Lord, I submit my future completely to you. I trust you. I don't care what kind of work you lead me to. I want to be a rushing stream, driven by you.*

CHAPTER 15

BACKFLIPS IN THE THRONE ROOM

I CAME OUT OF THE WILDERNESS revitalized and with a new depth of peace. Nothing in my circumstances had changed, but my internal world had shifted. It's easy to feel powerful when you have an awareness of God living inside of you. I would face the pain of this season with courage. I needed to mark this moment. I looked around the van. The drive home was quiet, with many of the guys trying to catch up on rest. I pulled my journal from the top of my pack and I began to write.

I am walking into a new season. I am not going to wait for a change in my circumstance, I am going to initiate change. I am going to be who I am, now. I am going to face opposition from rest, from worship, and from my communion with God. I am not a victim of circumstance, I make my circumstance subject to the Kingdom by making myself subject to the King. I refuse to wait to be rescued. You are here with me now.

I will lean into you, God, for strength and resolve, and I will face my giants head-on. Father, you are working here now. Give me eyes to see where you are moving so that I can join you. I know you are moving. I am going to move with you.

The next several months were an exercise in sheer trust. Each day I felt that I didn't have the capacity to do the things that were required of me, but I chose to trust that I had everything I needed. Living in a small community, it seemed I was daily running into reminders of disappointment and loss. Every time I saw people who had left our church—at the store, at The Depot, or on the road, the pain came rushing back. I learned to acknowledge the pain, to take a deep breath, and to loosen my grip. This was strength training.

My spirit—the part of me that was fully with Jesus, was growing stronger and more at the forefront. All the while my soul—the part of me that was daily reckoning with the painful emotions, was on a downward spiral of surrender. Several times a day I would whisper prayers of relinquishment, giving over to the Lord the world I had hoped to build. I learned to surrender what could have been, in order to embrace what was.

I began to notice a shift in our church. Every Sunday morning, I would look out at the continually shrinking crowd thinking, *are we even going to make it? Maybe we should close the doors and call it a day.* Then something would happen. God showed up in ways I never could have anticipated.

The timid Amish country mom would share a testimony that stirred boldness in the room. The tough farmer cried as he shared how he witnessed God's grace moving in the struggle of his dying brother. The factory worker who had been in bondage to so much shame became determined to put on a concert at the park, to bring hope to the community in the midst of a pandemic. The nursing student, who struggled with severe anxiety, who had been terrified to even step foot in the church, spontaneously shared a poem about the peace of God invading her turmoil.

There was a flow of grace in the room. People were speaking and moving with confidence that they were bringing something of value to the table. The sermon was no longer the pinnacle of the morning, and I was delightfully losing my status as the "expert." We were looking more and more like a body, each part owning its role and functioning without restriction. We were looking more and more like a family. A place of connection and safety where people could be real and raw, so that God's grace could freely flow into every crevice and valley that was opened to Him.

Week by week my jaw would drop as I witnessed church gatherings that reflected what God was putting in my own heart. In the most vulnerable moment of our church's history, God was stirring new expressions in our midst. Still, Melissa and I continued to suspect that there was a shift coming for our family. God had been cultivating a new grace in us, and there would be a new assignment.

Finally, that call came.

"Hey Putty! How's it going?" I put him on speakerphone so Melissa could join in.

"Oh it's good to hear your voice, friends!" He sighed as he said it. "It's going well. We're just tired from all the transition. We're looking forward to it being over!"

We had followed Putty from a distance for several years. He was a leader in our movement, passionate about equipping believers to live an empowered life in partnership with the Holy Spirit. He had surprised us all recently when he stepped down from his position in a large church. He left not knowing entirely what was next, but that the Lord was calling him to step out, to make space for a new assignment. He was working in an interim position in the meantime.

"We feel the same way. It's been a long season of transition with no end in sight."

"Well that's actually why I'm calling."

Melissa and I looked at each other, eyes wide. "What do you mean?"

"I know you guys know this, but I really believe that God is doing something different in the church."

"Yeah."

"Well, God is putting such a conviction in me that I have an assignment to be a church pioneer. I have some ideas and concepts that I'd like to try, and there's really no telling where it will go. Well, I think you guys have grace for it too, and I'd like for you to join me."

"Uh..." I didn't know what to say.

Melissa's jaw was dropped. "I think we have about a million questions right now."

"Me too." Putty laughed. "I'll tell you what I know, which isn't much. Based on the form of church I feel called to build, there most likely won't be paid positions. There are a few others who are considering it, we'll land in the same place and just build our team. We'll get on the same page on some basic convictions, then we'll experiment. Should be fun!"

"Where would we do this?" Melissa asked.

"I've been researching the right conditions for what we're building. It's going to be in Phoenix, Arizona."

Melissa stared at me with wild eyes as the conversation ended and I hung up the phone. "Are we *seriously* considering moving *across* the country, *with* children, *away from* all of our supports, to a place with a *significantly* higher cost of living, with *no prospect* of a job, and no clear plan?"

"I think so!" I flashed her a cheesy smile with gritted teeth.

We had been married long enough to know that when it came to risk, she was averse and I was addicted. When I saw a wild opportunity with unclear provision I became giddy, which was absolutely terrifying for her. But in this case, the Lord had made it clear to me that whatever was coming next for our family, Melissa would take the lead. She had hidden in the corner for a long time, but the Lord had slowly been drawing her out, creating such an internal safety with Him that she didn't need to hide.

She had been slowly coming out of hiding for the past few years, since we started SoKM. Now she was preaching, stepping into new roles and ministering to people one-on-one. I knew the Lord was only going to increase her influence, and I was excited to see where it would go. With every step in obedience, her heart was continually blooming. A move to Phoenix seemed just the right adventure for her, a next test for the depth of internal safety she had gained with God. But was it right for me?

I sat in my hidden corner of The Depot. I took a deep breath, feeling the warmth of my second mug of coffee. I put my headphones in, and the room around me disappeared. I closed my eyes and allowed the instrumental music to fill the canvas of my mind.

I saw myself underwater, rays of purple and blue light around me. I was doing back flips under the water. I popped my head through the surface, and I saw the open sea and sky in front of me. The water was perfectly calm, only my movement interrupted a sea of glass. The water must not have been too deep, because I dove and collected a few flat rocks. I came to the surface again, and tried skipping them across the water. I tried counting as the rocks skipped away, I laughed as they seemed to skip across endlessly.

I turned around and saw that there was an edge to the sea behind me, it was met by an ornate marble floor. The room was massive, seemingly stretching as far as the sea behind me. Near me was a large throne. When I saw it I wondered, *Is this God's throne room?* The answer wasn't clear, but I could tell He was near. When I feel His presence this strongly, there's always a strange combination of peace and energy.

As if on command, I went back to doing backflips in the water. Like a kid with his dad in the hotel pool, I was trying out a new skill in front of the Father. I had never really tried a backflip before, but it felt so right in the moment. There was a safety there, to try something I had never done.

The picture faded and I was back in the corner of The Depot. But the feelings persisted. God's nearness was so palpable that I began to tell Him what was on my heart. I grabbed my journal and initiated the conversation.

"Will I get to be who I am if we move to Phoenix?" The wording of the question surprised me, but I continued. "I've been discovering who I am with you Lord, and I quite like it. I have so many things that I'm doing right now that feel like such good expressions of who I am. I'm afraid that I'll lose those if we move, like there won't be space for them. But I want to make even more space for them! Can you promise that I won't lose these expressions?"

His nearness was so evident; it was easy to hear Him respond in my heart. "What if that's not what I have for you? Are you willing to lay these things down?"

Those questions stung. That wasn't the response I was expecting to hear from Him. "But Lord, you've been leading me in this process of discovering who I am and the grace that I carry. What's the point if you're going to rip those things out of my hands? Why would you dismiss the things that you put on my heart to begin with?"

"The longings you feel for those expressions are from Me, but the expressions become idols when you're not surrendered to me. I promise that I'll always fulfill those longings, but I can demand the expressions be surrendered whenever I choose. I will entrust to you even greater expressions when you prioritize your surrender over your reasoning. I want to entrust to you even greater expressions of who we are together. Do you trust me?"

I didn't feel the need to answer Him. The question weighed on me, and I needed to sit with what He was saying. *What if we move to Phoenix, and I have to work a job that doesn't fit who I am? I've been in ministry for all of my adult life, would I be satisfied working behind a desk, so Melissa can do an experimental church with a team? What if the financial demands of the city are so high that I'm enslaved to work, and I never get to escape to the wilderness?*

God was not promising that I would get to continue to do the things that I loved, in fact it seemed He was promising that I wouldn't. I couldn't picture these *better expressions* He had promised; I could only see the cost. I needed to get my feet on the ground in Phoenix to get a better vantage point.

CHAPTER 16

GAINING ALTITUDE

AT AN ALTITUDE OF 34,000 FEET, I leaned back in my seat and closed my eyes. The constant hum of the plane provided a nice background, canceling out the world around me. I asked the Lord, "Would you come and meet me here?"

As I took a deep breath, a picture began to form in my mind. I was sitting on the wing of a small plane in flight. I tightly gripped the front edge of the wing beneath me. Despite knowing I wasn't actually in danger, I was tense. The landscape below resembled the southwest: canyons, dispersed across the desert. To my right was the cockpit, to my left sat Jesus.

He was looking at me, smiling. He was completely at rest, baggy clothes blowing in the wind. When I saw Him so relaxed, I relaxed. I leaned my head into His chest and He held me. I closed my eyes, allowing myself to feel the safety of his arms around me. Eventually I noticed a glow coming from His chest. I pulled back to inspect. In bright red letters was the word, TRUST, imprinted on His chest.

Over the years I've grown to admire this about Jesus. He trusted the Father, completely, absolutely, perfectly. He had an unshakeable trust in the heart and the care of the Father. It was no wonder He could sleep in a sinking boat in a wild storm. The wing of a plane was no different.

He saw me, admiring the word. He took His hand and placed it on His chest. Then He slowly moved His hand from His chest to mine. He pressed His hand into my chest and held it there for a moment. Then He pulled it away.

I looked down. In bright, red letters, the word "trust" was imprinted on my chest. I began to cry. I could feel the shape and the weight of the word through my whole body. Jesus laughed. Then He leaned over the front edge of the wing, lifted His hands in front of Him, and rolled off.

In light of the glow on my chest, His action wasn't at all odd to me. It was like I saw it coming, and there was no hesitation to follow Him. I rolled off right behind Him. Together we took in the beauty below as we moved toward the earth. The desert was full of various shades of red and brown. Light reflected off of the mountains and canyons. I can't begin to describe the depth of peace I experienced, free-falling through the sky.

As the ground began to approach, I thought, "I wonder how He's going to work this out..."

As if in response, Jesus wrapped himself around me from behind. Suddenly I was wearing a wingsuit. I had seen videos of people wearing these with such jealousy. Now Jesus had just become one around me!

I aimed for a large canyon to my right. I flew through the canyon at rapid speed. "Yeeeeeaaaaa!" I yelled in my imagination.

The plane began its descent and I was back in my seat. How awesome was that? I couldn't wait to brag to Melissa that I had been skydiving with Jesus. The Lord was cultivating deeper and deeper trust in me, and a real transaction had just taken place. The glow of my chest was gone, but I could feel its impact still.

As the plane taxied to the gate, I turned my phone off of airplane mode. Immediately my phone buzzed with notifications. Deb had texted me.

Hey Kyle! This morning I was praying for you and your trip out west. As I was praying, the Lord gave me two pictures. The first was of you guys in Aurora. You were financially secure with insurance, but you were miserable. The second was a picture of you in Phoenix. You were surrounded by mountains, on an adventure without financial security, but you were having the time of your lives.

Then the Lord asked me, "Which would you choose for them? Which do you think I want for them?" I've got to be honest, I've been fearful about all the risks you'd face in Phoenix, but my answer was obviously Phoenix. Then the Lord responded, "Okay, then trust me and pray with faith, not worry."

My neighbor nudged me, "Looks like it's our turn," he said with a smile.

"Oh, sorry!" I grabbed my stuff and exited the plane.

It had been two months since our conversation with Putty, and it had been fourteen months since our discernment had really begun with the email from Aurora. For so long I just wanted God to tell me what to do. I remembered my conversation with Andy that night where the two tributaries came together. *Sons can't mature unless they're given freedom and power to make decisions*. There of course would always be moments where God would give a clear direction. But this wouldn't be one of those times. He was trusting me to choose in a way that reflects and reveals Him.

Being entrusted with a high-level decision is a scary thing. The weight of the consequences can make you cautious to trust any thought. As I drove though Phoenix, I was invigorated by the environment. Literally every single direction I looked there were mountains. They seemed to create an electric force field causing energy to course through me. Was I really capable of being objective in this environment?

After a full day of travel and exploring the metropolis, I crashed at the Airbnb. My body hadn't adjusted to the time change, so I woke up at 4:45 a.m. I decided I'd take advantage of my early start, and climb a mountain in time to watch the sunrise. After flipping my eggs and downing a cup of coffee, I looked up *hiking near me.* The options were endless. I picked a butte fifteen minutes away, filled my water bottle, and headed out before five-thirty.

I pulled into the parking lot, surprised to see several early-morning hikers. At the trailhead there was a box full of bananas with a note saying, "Help yourselves!" *Thanks, mysterious host.* I grabbed a banana and headed up the trail.

Fairly quickly, the trail became very steep. Over a little more than a mile I'd climbed 1,200 feet of elevation. Some spots were so steep; I was climbing boulders to follow the trail. I couldn't believe I could find a hike this challenging within the city.

As I hiked, I remembered what I had felt as we drove into Aurora. I recalled the moment as I stopped at a vista on the side of the trail.

Here, I could look out for miles in every direction and see mountains. Buildings of all shapes and sizes lay below—all of them tiny from here. In the midst of the city was a wild and living desert. It was as though the city and the wilderness had agreed to cohabitate. There were cacti in every direction. The red dirt provided a shared backdrop as it gleamed in the rising sun. Some places you could see a butte (which is like a small mountain), popping up between skyscrapers.

The scenery on the drive into Aurora was such a contrast to

this place. From the road I could see for miles because everything was so flat. All I could see was a sea of cornfields in every direction. To some, such a sight was majestic. I could understand how others would see beauty, but to me it was dull. As I considered moving to such a space, I felt sick to my stomach.

Sometimes I fall into the trap of believing that I'm not allowed to want anything, as if our desires are in constant opposition to what God wants for us. But the truth is more nuanced than we'd like. It would be easy to simply say that our desires are always for evil, because then we wouldn't have to live in the gray.

But if we're truly a new creation in Christ, then our truest desires align with God's heart. We haven't yet learned to live from our truest selves, so we're in process. We can learn to pay attention to our desires, bringing them before the Lord.

Shame tells us to stuff them down so as not to expose our brokenness. But personally I find that even when I bring an impure desire before the Lord, He doesn't condemn me. Instead He teaches me to honor my longing, and to find my deepest fulfillment in Him.

I had taken note of the ache in my stomach as I surveyed the flat landscape as we approached Aurora. I'd vowed to the Lord, "If you are calling us here, I'll do it. And I'm confident that if this is where you're leading us, it will be good. But, Lord, is there any chance you could call me to a place with mountains instead?"

It had felt like a silly and selfish prayer at the time. I wouldn't let my love for the mountains trump my desire to follow the Lord.

Now, I marveled as I stood to the side of the trail, overlooking downtown Phoenix. Beyond the city was another row of mountains. In every direction I looked, I saw mountains in the distance. A warm wave moved through my body as I sensed the Lord's pleasure over me. As if in response to my prayer back in Aurora, I could hear the Lord's whisper in my heart.

"I could do that for you."

EPILOGUE

I STOOD IN THE AISLE, bracing my chin with clenched jaw. My stomach became unsettled as the price tags glared back at me. The echoes of a busy store rang around me as I examined the various paint sprayers. No matter what I chose I would be spending some precious cash.

Five days ago, we moved into our rental in Gurnee, Illinois. Ultimately we're still heading to Phoenix, Arizona, but we decided to join our team in Illinois for a season of training and preparation before we head to Phoenix. I have officially walked away from my sixteen-year career in vocational ministry, and I am building a handyman business.

I moved to Illinois with no work scheduled. I was terrified. If I'm honest, I still am. In the last few days I've been driving all over Chicago suburbs running estimates. As I ran estimates, it became clear there were some tools I'd need to add to my arsenal. It's scary, spending even more money when income isn't guaranteed.

In a back corner of Menards, I said a simple prayer. "Jesus please get us through this."

As if in direct response I was reminded of what the Lord had said when I was installing the water heater (chapter 3). "You're not doing this to provide, that's my job. You're doing this because I made you like me, your work is an expression of who you are." I took a breath as the tension left my jaw. A smile formed as I remembered my situation.

I don't have to be afraid. God is providing for me every step of the way. I grabbed the paint sprayer that seemed to fit my needs and headed for more supplies.

This experience earlier today only reinforces why I wrote this book. Our experiences with God are a living testimony. Sure, they testify to other people, but more importantly they are a testimony to us. Just as God revealed himself to us through Jesus, He is continually revealing Himself to us through the Holy Spirit in our everyday lives.

When we choose to tune in and perceive Him, it's an invitation into an adventure with God. Sometimes these are big invitations, but more often they are small and subtle. Either way, every time we respond in trust, something important is cultivated in us and it becomes a building block for future adventures. Our history with God is meant to become a stunning mosaic, in which forms shift and patterns emerge, and upon colliding with other patterns, they continually create beauty and meaning.

You're on a journey, and its trajectory has a much more significant impact on the world around you than you're aware. The more fully you can step into an awareness of God's presence with you, the more equipped you are for your journey. You can learn to cultivate an intimate connection with Him and to navigate daily challenges and decisions with Him in a way that immerses your world in His goodness.

May you personally discover the God who is *with you*.

KYLE PETERS

Kyle and Melissa Peters live in Gurnee, Illinois with their two kids (Micah and Elise), where they are preparing to plant an experimental expression of church in Phoenix, Arizona. Along with the rest of the team they're working with, they believe that the Church in their lifetime is going through a significant transition, and that they are called to be pioneers in the process. Currently, Kyle serves as a handyman, partnering with the Spirit to improve homes and to minister the love of Jesus to homeowners.

Kyle is an adventurer and a storyteller. He has served as an associate pastor and senior pastor over the last sixteen years, led wilderness trips, and facilitated inner healing work with individuals and groups in partnership with Healing Care.

His passion is to help others cultivate a lifestyle of intimacy with God and to take risks in advancing the Kingdom of God. He has traveled across the country as a speaker and trainer for inner healing and kingdom equipping.

Connect with Kyle at TopoWilderness.com.

Help other readers find books that they'll love by leaving an honest review of this book at Amazon.com or Goodreads.com

www.ingramcontent.com/pod-product-compliance
Lightning Source LLC
Chambersburg PA
CBHW022106040426
42451CB00007B/141
9781960230003